Look Out, Doctor!

DR ROBERT CLIFFORD

Illustrated by NICK BAKER

SPHERE BOOKS LIMITED

SPHERE BOOKS LTD

Penguin Books Ltd, 27 Wrights Lane, London W8 5TZ (Publishing and Editorial)
and Harmondsworth, Middlesex, England (Distribution and Warehouse)
Viking Penguin Inc., 40 West 23rd Street, New York, New York 10010, USA
Penguin Books Australia Ltd, Ringwood, Victoria, Australia
Penguin Books Canada Ltd, 2801 John Street, Markham, Ontario, Canada L3R 1B4
Penguin Books (NZ) Ltd, 182–190 Wairau Road, Auckland 10, New Zealand

First published in Great Britain by Pelham Books Ltd 1983
Published by Sphere Books Ltd 1984
Reprinted 1985, 1986, 1987

Printed and bound in Great Britain by
Cox & Wyman Ltd, Reading

Still on the trail of sugar, I gave him a blood sample bottle with an envelope to take to the hospital, for a blood test, and a bottle to take to the surgery to fill with a specimen of urine. He returned in a few minutes announcing his return by banging on the door with his knees. When I opened the door, I found him precariously supporting a urine-filled envelope in both hands. The blood and urine sample bottles were both in his top pocket.

It was going to be one of those days.

For Steve, Hewie, Fred, Stan, Joan and Pam,
who put up with me, for so many happy years

Contents

	Prologue	9
1	It's Not Cricket	11
2	The Kiss of Life	22
3	Going Off With a Bang	31
4	Normally Abnormal	43
5	Holidays With the Family	56
6	Rewarding Years	66
7	Pearls Before Swine	76
8	Ways of Dying	88
9	A Fate Worse than Death	107
10	Trouble at Mill	118
11	Changing Times	125
12	Letter from America	133
13	Diets and Boat Trips	142
14	First Pike	153
15	Leaving the Nest	162
	Postscript	168

Prologue

Life is a tragedy, for we are all born eventually to die. We survive our tragedies by laughing at them.

A friend once told me that when he was under the influence of ether he dreamed he was turning over the pages of a great book, in which he knew he would find, on the last page, the meaning of life.

The pages of the book were alternately tragic and comic, and he turned page after page, his excitement growing, not only because he was approaching the answer, but because he couldn't know, until he arrived, on which side of the book the final page would be. At last it came: the universe opened up to him in a hundred words: and they were uproariously funny.

He came back to consciousness crying with laughter, remembering everything. He opened his lips to speak. It was then that the great and comic answer plunged back out of his reach.

Christopher Fry

CHAPTER 1

It's Not Cricket

My first patient in the surgery was Benny Talbot, a tall, gangly
youth with a prime crop of acne pustules and mini-boils scat-
tered at random over his body.

Excess sugar in the blood could have been one reason for the
spots and boils, so I asked if he suffered from thirst (a positive
symptom in recognising sugar diabetes). He told me that he was
often so thirsty on a Saturday night that he had been known to
down ten pints of beer at the Tadchester Arms. Not quite what I
meant: a symptom like that would mean that half the young
men of Tadchester were diabetic.

An undiagnosed diabetic can be so thirsty that he will drink
the contents of his hot water bottle in the middle of the night.
My spotty patient did not admit to ever having been so
tempted. He did, however, remember that he sometimes had to
get up in the night to pass water, and on close questioning, he
did think this was probably Saturday nights.

Still on the trail of sugar, I gave him a blood sample bottle
with an envelope to take to the hospital, for a blood test, and a
bottle to take to the surgery toilet to fill with a specimen of urine.

He returned in a few minutes, announcing his return by
banging on the door with his knees. When I opened the door, I

found him precariously supporting a urine-filled envelope in both hands. The blood and urine sample bottles were both in his top pocket.

It was going to be one of those days.

My second patient was John Haggard, a well-groomed, nicely spoken man of about thirty-five. His hair was neat, his shoes shining, and he had sharp creases to his trousers. He was wearing a good, but rather old, grey-striped city suit. He looked immaculate, and it was only on closer inspection that minor blemishes of dress became apparent. His shirt, though clean and starched, had started to fray at the collar. His tie, which was a club or regimental tie, was slightly worn at the knot.

He was a little apprehensive and had an air of gentleness about him that warmed me to him.

He was not a patient I knew — he had filled in a temporary resident's card — and I noted that his parents came from an unpretentious home in Stowin. His home address was that of a Midlands hospital whose name was familiar but which I couldn't place immediately. My guess was that he was a hospital administrator, in Tadchester on holiday at his parents'.

He began hesitantly: 'I would be so grateful if you could help me, Doctor. A few years ago I had a nervous breakdown and was admitted to hospital. Happily I made a good recovery and for the last ten years I have run the clerical side of the hospital.' (I was pleased with my spot prognosis of a hospital administrator.)

'This has suited me so far, but I have now been offered a better post in London. I am in the ridiculous situation of never having been officially discharged as a patient. To do so I have to get my next of kin to vouch for me. I popped down here to get my parents to sign the appropriate forms, and I can't persuade them to sign. They are simple folk and don't trust forms. Could you possibly speak to them, and reassure them on my behalf?'

His story was odd but quite plausible. Many patients in mental hospitals rehabilitated themselves by helping out in various administrative tasks, and this chap was obviously quite all right.

I vaguely knew his parents. His father ran the secondhand furniture auctions for Hope's Stores and his mother worked as a cleaner at one of the hotels. They were from the Midlands and had moved down to Tadchester about ten years previously, but they had kept very much to themselves, never really integrating into Tadchester's way of life.

There was an air of quiet desperation about the young man and I impulsively agreed to speak on his behalf.

'Today, Doctor?'

'Yes,' I said, slightly intimidated by his persistence. 'I will pop in and see your parents this evening.'

'Thank you, Doctor. Thank you, Doctor,' he replied, almost fawningly. I began to go off him.

The rest of the day continued in its uneasy and unsatisfactory pattern. At home the children were all beginning to go down with colds, and even the nose of Susie, our Cairn terrier, was disturbingly warm.

My wife Pam was her usual patient, unruffable self. So I cheered up a bit during supper and set off for the Haggards' to intercede on their son's behalf.

The Haggards lived in a bungalow perched in the middle of a two-acre orchard near the riverside village of Stowin. The property was surrounded by a high wooden fence and in the dark of a March evening I could make out trimmed lawns and neatly clipped trees.

The door was opened by Mr Haggard.

'Hello, Doctor. This is a surprise,' he said. 'What can I do for you?'

'I've called to talk to you about your son,' I replied.

'Oh, God! What has he done now?' wailed Mrs Haggard in the background.

'You'd better come in,' said Mr Haggard darkly.

I was shown into the front room: settee in the corner, aspidistra in shining copper bowl in the window, and tall, hard-backed chairs arranged round a shiny pedestal table. In the middle of the table lay a fat family Bible with a huge metal clasp on its side.

I was summoned to sit down at one end of the table while Mr Haggard sat at the other. It was like being called to a board meeting.

Mr Haggard lowered his head as if to start our meeting with a prayer. Suddenly he looked up and shouted, 'Look out, Doctor!'

I shot out of my chair just in time to miss a cricket bat smashing down on the top of the back of it.

Standing wild-eyed, brandishing the bat, was my well-groomed and nicely spoken patient of the morning.

I acted instinctively. I turned and hurled myself at him head-down, as if I were going into a rugby scrum. The whole weight of my body was behind my head, which slammed into his solar plexus and pinned him to the wall.

I stood back and he fell into a breathless heap on the floor. I was taking no chances: I jumped on him and held his head in a lock. He had unleashed some primitive force in me, and if I'd carried on I could have killed him.

I was conscious of Mr Haggard pulling on my sleeve.

'It's all right, Doctor,' he said. 'You can leave him alone. He won't hurt anyone now.'

As soon as I let go, the son curled himself up in a ball and lay weeping at the foot of the wall. Several hours, several policemen and two duly authorised officers later, Master Haggard was on his way back to the Midlands hospital, which I now remembered was a hospital for the criminally insane.

The sad story was that the Haggard son, who was normal most of the time, had occasional brain storms during which he became physically violent.

He had an intense grudge against doctors. It was after he had cracked the skull of a doctor in the Midlands that he was incarcerated in hospital and his parents moved to Tadchester.

Things were not sorted out until the early hours of the morning. As I drove back along the Winchcombe Road the car started to lurch.

I stopped and got out. The back tyre was flat.

It had definitely been one of those days.

*　　*　　*

I was the fourth partner in a group of five in a little Somerset town called Tadchester. Tadchester (population 6,500) stands on the estuary of the River Tad, in one of the most beautiful parts of the Somerset coast. It is a market town, with some fishing, some light industry, and a great deal of farming.

The town is split in two by the River Tad, and further split by the large hill which dominates one side of the river. The other side of the river is flat pastureland, stretching off to marshes and the sea coast. You are not just a Tadchester resident — you are strictly Up-the-Hill or Down-the-Hill. It has important social distinction: the population Up-the-Hill tends to be the Have-nots.

We were the only general practice in the town, and also took

15

care of the local hospital. The five partners each had his own area of responsibility at the hospital: Steve Maxwell, the senior partner, had a special interest in medicine; Henry Johnson, the second senior, was the surgeon; Jack Hart, the third partner, was the anaesthetist; I, as the fourth partner, was reckoned to be the expert on midwifery and was pretty good at piercing ears; and Ron Dickinson, the fifth and junior partner — an accomplished athlete who spent a great deal of his time running, jumping, swimming, sailing, water ski-ing, etc. — was our ENT specialist and removed the local tonsils. We were a happy and well-balanced team.

One of the delights of Tadchester was that it was one of the few British ports where the quay was clean and fresh, where unloading ships were not surrounded by dirt and railway tracks. The coasters that came from Scandinavia, France and Belgium with loads of coal, timber and clay would always unload tidily onto a string of lorries on the quay.

You could while away a pleasant afternoon sitting on a bench by the quay, watching the ships unloading and the salmon fishermen shooting their seine nets. Two or three fishing boats still went out of Tadchester, and landing craft, from the school of amphibious warfare at the mouth of the Tad, would often appear on exercises. These squat grey boxes would come charging up the river followed by men in tiny boats, all in camouflage green. Even these seemed to blend in with the surroundings.

Work prevented me from taking frequent strolls around the town, but three or four times a year on a Saturday morning, I would make a point of doing what almost amounted to a grand tour.

I would start at the top of the High Street, parking my car behind the black and white chip shop, by the grace and favour of Jack and Lesley Morris, the owners. I would then walk down the High Street, passing a few small shops before branching off right to the pannier market, where dozens of individual stalls sold vegetables, cream, eggs, chickens, potatoes and bric-à-brac. I knew most of the stallholders and it was very much like doing a ward round. My mind had to race to connect every condition with every recognisable face and not confuse the ailments with the names. A complete circuit of the market, then down to the bottom of the High Street, passing the new Woolworth, Hope's Stores, a mini department store that had been there since 1699, round The Globe pub on the corner, then a cup of coffee at the Copper Inn, which was directly on the quay just downstream of the bridge.

From the Copper Inn one could see most things that were going on in the town and on a Saturday morning everybody who was anybody met for coffee. There would be JPs, councillors, doctors, solicitors — all representatives of the hierarchy which ran the town. This was where business deals were done and had been done for 500 years.

Running parallel to the quay were Milk Lane and Rope Lane, narrow streets honeycombed with shops, like primitive shopping precincts. In years gone by there had been a rope factory off Rope Lane and the bollards on which the ropes were stretched still stood at either end of this narrow street. I expect at one time there had been a dairy in Milk Lane, but it was all gift shops now.

On my tours I would wander down Rope Lane, which linked the High Street with Bridge Street, and pop into the electrical shop owned by my very good friend Eric Martin, for a yarn. Then onto the quay again to meander round the park, the children's putting green, Humber Memorial Art Gallery and Museum and back along the broad street that swept off the quay, along the eastern edge of the town, passing the Hambrose Garage and the Regal Cinema, then up Pitt Lane to the top of the High Street.

Everyone I passed was always very friendly, and I would sometimes be offered jobs like cleaning fish or washing dishes.

'Come on, Doctor Bob,' someone would shout. 'Give up doctoring and have a go at this for a change.'

I think I made these trips to reassure myself. I knew most of the people in the town but usually saw them from the other side of the surgery desk, when they were not feeling at their best. It was very refreshing to see them in different circumstances, and it certainly helped when I was feeling a bit down.

All in all, we had a good town.

*　　*　　*

Every summer, invading holidaymakers strained the local medical services to the limit, and Tadchester people much resented sharing their medical facilities with foreigners.

Illness on holiday is much worse than illness at home. Not only is the holiday ruined for the patients — lying staring at a ward ceiling instead of enjoying the sea air and scenery — but also for their relatives and friends who spend much of their time in waiting rooms hoping for news.

Death on holiday — though obviously no happy event for the patient — is extra harrowing for the relatives or friends who have to make complicated arrangements to have the body transported back home.

Only a very small proportion of the visitors fell ill, of course, but as they took up so much of our working day we forgot that the other 99·5 per cent were healthy and thoroughly enjoying themselves.

Ironically, the seriously ill were the least trouble: they went straight into hospital. The biggest problems were the patients who were not well enough to cope in their holiday accommodation and therefore had to be looked after.

My partner Henry used to come into his own with cases like these. Although principally a surgeon, Henry, aided by Jack Hart, also had under his charge the Fever Hospital that perched on top of the hill in Tadchester.

The hospital had four large wards, which in the days when tuberculosis and other infectious diseases were very serious, were always full. As antibiotics dealt with these problems, so the hospital gradually emptied.

Only a skeleton staff was kept on, and just two of the wards were open. I think there was some vague scheme to use the hospital fully in the event of an atomic war, but to all intents and purposes this was now Henry's private hospital.

He would take in convalescent patients, or elderly people whose children needed a rest from caring for them, and in the summer he took in most of the semi-hospital cases needing care and attention. Henry was the final arbiter on admissions. I could never assume that I might admit patients in my own right and, though I could visit them, could play no part in their treatment.

One such patient was Herbert Bagley. He had come down with a group of lads from Bath to stay at the local holiday camp at Sanford-on-Sea, and was taken ill with a very sore throat. The sore throat didn't settle down and didn't respond to antibiotics. A blood test showed that he had glandular fever.

Herbert had an awful time. He had glandular fever at its worst with every possible complication: high fever, jaundice, inability to eat, vomiting and excruciating soreness of the throat. He was in hospital just over a month and I used to visit him every couple of days and try to cheer him up.

He was a handsome, likeable lad with a great big frame. His strong arms were tattooed with 'I Love Hazel' on the left and a crown and anchor on the right. Perched on his locker was a large photograph of a scowling girl with short hair and big thighs, sitting astride a dropped-handlebar racing bike.

'That's what keeps me going,' he said. 'That's my Hazel. We're getting married next spring.'

Though I would never have said it, I thought that he could have done better than the baleful Amazon in the photo.

Within a week of Herbert's being discharged, I was called to Sanford-on-Sea again to see another lad, Sid Parker. He had an exact replica of Herbert's symptoms and glandular fever was diagnosed again. He passed Henry's scrutiny and was admitted to the Fever Hospital. Again, I used to visit him every other day.

On my second visit I noticed propped up on his locker a large photograph of a glowering, short-haired girl with large thighs, sitting astride a dropped-handlebar racing bike.

I was about to say 'Oh, I'm afraid the last patient must have left this behind,' when some instinct stopped me.

'Who's the lady?' I asked.

'That's my Hazel,' said Sid. 'We're getting married in the spring.'

I made no comment. There wasn't a lot I could say, anyway.

Glandular fever is sometimes called the kissing disease. It is thought that one of the ways it spreads is by mouth-to-mouth contact. If both these lads had pursued Hazel and were contemplating marrying her next spring, then it was likely that they had been kissing her. So it was likely that Hazel was the cause of Herbert and Sid finishing up in hospital.

Sid came from Clevedon, south of Bristol. He was quite different from Herbert: small and neat, had some good 'A' levels and was waiting for a university place. Again, a likeable lad. And again, I thought he could have done better than Hazel.

The nurses were completely loyal and, apart from an occasional quiet snigger, didn't give the secret away.

Sid got better in three weeks and went home. We were left with the mystery of one boy from Bath and one boy from Clevedon, both sublimely confident that they were going to marry this cross-looking, hefty cyclist in the following spring.

We had a busier year than usual with holidaymakers. Two outbreaks of gastro-enteritis at the holiday camp absolutely packed the Fever Hospital, and the memory of Sid and Herbert was submerged in the avalanche of work.

The family and I took our holiday late that year. We hired a villa on the western coast of France below the Sable de Lonne, took a ferry to Cherbourg and then motored leisurely down over two or three days.

We spent our first night in the most beautiful town of Vitre where, it seemed, every other building was a church, and booked in at a quaint old hotel. Both the proprietor and his wife were charming and we were immediately adopted by their twenty-year-old son, Ernst, who was anxious to use his English and learn about England.

Ernst had an English fiancée whom he was going to marry next spring. We congratulated him and invited him to call on us in England.

'I will get you a photograph of her,' he said. He rushed up to his room and came down with the now familiar photograph of a scowling, short-haired, thick-thighed girl straddling a dropped-handlebar racing bike.

'This is 'Azel,' said Ernst. 'I look forward to bringing her to you after we are married.'

I still wonder about the power of this girl with the thick thighs, unprepossessing face and dropped handlebars. Three men were proposing to marry her in the spring — and those were only the ones I'd met. Were they just the tip of the iceberg? Were there dozens of men all over Europe who were confidently planning to settle down with Hazel (or 'Azel)? What was the secret of her attraction? What was her special magic? Certainly, if she could bottle it, she'd make a fortune.

I tried to find out whether Ernst had had glandular fever, but neither his English nor my French were up to it.

'Have you had a fever?' I asked.

'Yes,' he replied. 'I love her very much. Always I am in fever.'

It was stalemate.

Ernst never arrived with his blushing (or scowling) bride, nor did we even hear from him afterwards.

For Pam and myself, Hazel joined the Mona Lisa as one of the world's most enigmatic women — though she, poor girl, was definitely no oil painting.

CHAPTER 2

The Kiss of Life

For some reason I could never understand, the number of people who wished to visit the surgery steadily increased in number year by year, although the population of Tadchester was almost static. The number of residents had even fallen a little bit after the closure of the coal mine but then picked up as the plastics and electronics factories got underway.

As we had an appointments system we were actually able to count how many people attended. If we weren't careful we could easily be overrun.

I don't think that people came unnecessarily: just being worried is reason enough to go and see your doctor, however stupid the worry. Worry is a debilitating, exhausting business. If you think that spot on your face is cancer and you've made your will and visualised your funeral, you will go on worrying until someone has reassured you.

We were fortunate in our surgery staff. Practice manager was the fierce Gladys who had been our senior receptionist for so long that she thought of it as *her* practice. When I first came to Tadchester I remember overhearing her telling some friends that she now had another doctor to train. But she had a heart of gold. Under her stern exterior there was, in fact, a very human

person, highly capable of distinguishing the wheat from the chaff. She had to screen people coming in, otherwise we would have been overwhelmed.

Our other watchdog was the inimitable Grace, much more newly arrived than Gladys.

Grace got away with everything with sheer audacity. She had the art of saying the most outrageous things without being offensive.

An over-weight businessman trying to make a surgery appointment with Grace would be met with, 'What is it you want, love? The maternity clinic?'

Although other staff came and went, Gladys and Grace were permanent fixtures. As well as this they were great buddies. Completely different personalities, they somehow gelled as a pair, and at weekends you would see them together walking their dogs along the beach at Sanford-on-Sea.

Grace was irrepressible. She could have made her living as a stand-up comic. The only time I have ever known the wind taken out of her sails was when a patient fell in love with her.

She was happily married to Jack, a mechanic who worked at one of the Tadchester garages.

Her admirer was a tiny gentleman, a Mr Wood who had a photographic shop down on the quay. His courtship started with a number of small presents he brought with him when he came to the surgery.

His visits were frequent. He came to see me with a whole lot of bizarre complaints, none of which was important, but he was prepared to sit discussing them for hours.

Each time he came he brought Grace some little offering: chocolates, a bottle of wine, or flowers.

'Just a small expression of my appreciation,' he would say, looking earnestly at Grace. 'You're so kind to me and you are so good to us all here.'

At first Grace was flattered. She called Jack Wood 'Tom Thumb'. As he was only about five foot three, I don't think he would have liked that. As the weeks went by it became steadily embarrassing. He would arrive at the surgery an hour early for his appointment and sit in the chair facing the reception desk, glancing devotedly at Grace. The normally boisterous Grace became quieter and quieter.

'Blimey,' she said when he had gone, 'I feel I can go and get dressed again now.'

He used to hang about outside the surgery offering to take her home, but Grace usually found some excuse.

It came to a head one day when Grace set off for home in the most appalling driving wind and rain.

A car pulled up with a *whoosh*! and the door was flung open. Grace would have accepted a lift from anyone that day.

'I had only just got in the bloody car,' she said, 'when I felt a hand on my knee. "You can put that back on the wheel," I said. "It's no good trying to steer with my knees."'

'I'm sorry, Grace,' said Mr Wood. 'I wouldn't offend you for the world, I just wanted to be friendly. It's my mission in life to try and make people happy. Are you happy, Grace? Could I make you happier?'

'Didn't know what to say,' said Grace, 'I was sweating all over.'

At this stage she was so furious she hadn't realised that instead of driving home he had drawn up outside his photographic shop.

'I said to him, "What are we doing here?"'

'Well,' said Mr Wood, 'you must know how much I admire you. I want to take you to my room above the shop where we could physically and mentally commune. I think making love is one of the best medicines in life. I think it's helpful for people and I do like to help people.'

The hand reached again for her knee.

'By this time,' said Grace, 'I was really fighting mad. I hit him under the chin with my right elbow and his head went back and hit the side of the door.

'"You can just bugger off," I told him. "After you've got hold of that steering wheel and driven me home."'

'I could cope with that little bugger,' she said. 'I wasn't going to walk back in the storm.'

They drove home in silence. When they reached her gate the crestfallen Mr Wood said, 'Is there no hope?'

'You go back to your shop and jump into your developing tank,' said Grace. 'When you've grown another foot come back and ask me again.'

The next day in the surgery Grace was back to her old rip-roaring self.

Miraculously Mr Wood recovered from all the numerous minor ailments that he had been consulting me about. And Grace, though she made us all laugh about the story of her admirer, was secretly quite pleased that a man had found her so desirable.

Our nickname for Grace had always been Amazing Grace, but from then on we got into the habit of calling her Sexy Grace. And it stuck.

*   *   *

Gladys was the commandant of the local Red Cross society. When I first came to Tadchester, she enrolled me as medical officer to the Tadchester Forward Medical Aid Unit. We used to race round the country taking part in competitions dealing with mass 'casualties', in the sort of numbers you'd expect if there was a nuclear war. The Government decided that these competitions were too expensive to run and after achieving great heights — we reached the national finals at the Albert Hall in front of the Minister of Health — the Tadchester Forward Medical Aid Unit was disbanded.

I had by now, though, earned a reputation as a first aider and spent a great deal of my time teaching the methods involved, writing instructional pamphlets, examining first-aid test candidates, and taking part in demonstrations. I was chatting about this one morning at coffee with Henry, Steve, Jack and Ron. Coffee time was when we got our worries off our chests, and it really was a very important part of the practice. If we had anxieties we would share them with our partners, and I was indeed fortunate with my colleagues.

'God,' I said, 'I'm so fed up with first aid. Pam says I'm even waking her in the night trying to give her mouth-to-mouth resuscitation.'

'I've heard it called worse,' said Jack.

Steve Maxwell looked over his half-rimmed glasses.

'You haven't been in the practice long enough, Bob, to remember Miss Polly Fulton,' he said.

'For twenty years I gave the first-aid lectures to Tadchester Red Cross and for twenty years Polly Fulton came and attended — and she was a good seventy when she started. She sat at the back of the class, always asked a question on shock and to my knowledge never ever participated in any practical first aid. She was never seen wearing her uniform at football matches, fetes or cinemas. I thought all my tuition had been wasted until one day I met her in Bridge Street. She came up excitedly and said "Dr Maxwell! Dr Maxwell! At last my first aid has been useful. There was a terrible accident on the Hovery Road yesterday. Three cars piled up, there were fractured arms and fractured legs, amputated limbs. It was absolutely terrible!''

'''I'm glad you were there,'' I said. "What did you do? Put on splints and tourniquets, dial 999?''

'''Oh no, nothing like that,'' said Miss Polly Fulton. "But if I hadn't known to put my head between my knees I would have fainted...'''

* * *

Henry was never lost for words. Not to be out-done, he went on to tell his first story.

'I was examining these young farmer chaps in their first aid,' he said. 'They don't know very much, so I kept the questions fairly basic. I said to this young lad, "If you saw a pretty girl lying face downwards in a stream what would you do?"

'''Well,'' said the young farmer, "I'd jump into the stream.''

'''Good,'' I said.

'''Pull her to the bank.''

'''Good,'' I said.

'''Loosen her clothing.''

'''Good,'' I said.

'''And then,'' said the farmer, "I'd start giving her artificial insemination.'''

Steve roared.

'I pass,' said Jack Hart.

'The only thing I can think of,' said Ron Dickinson, 'was that I once had trouble teaching a man mouth-to-mouth resuscitation. I knew it was going to be tricky when I had to make him take his cigarette out of his mouth before I started...'

* * *

As the years went by we had to make additions to the surgery. We were now no longer just a general practice, we had grown into a health centre, with health visitors, district nurses, social workers, even psychiatric social workers. There seemed an unending stream of extra staff.

Rooms accumulated, were turned into such things as

chiropody clinics and eye clinics, and much of the intimate atmosphere of the surgery was lost.

I found the work of district nurses and health visitors invaluable. They were dedicated women, often doing the most menial of jobs, and were able to reduce our workload quite a bit.

Social workers tended to remain aloof from us. They did their own thing and there was never enough cooperation. A tremendous amount of time seemed to be spent in case conferences and writing reports. We reckoned that one doctor working hard for a full day would cover the work of all the social workers in the Tadchester area for a week.

I don't think it was their fault. They didn't really have too many powers and they couldn't allocate beds of their own. Among the auxiliary helpers, they really were the odd men out, and we felt that the whole social work position ought to be re-appraised.

One addition that proved especially useful to the care of patients at home was the increasing scope of the occupational therapist. I had always thought of occupational therapists as ladies who taught you how to do tapestry, solve jigsaws, knit and crochet rugs, but this new breed of determined young women were like engineers. They could have bungalows built or adapted for the handicapped, they would fix up all sorts of home aids, and to two of my patients particularly they gave a completely new lease of life.

Dr Jacqueline Dean, a medical colleague, was a walking museum of pathology. She had liver trouble, bone trouble, blood trouble, bowel trouble, and had been bedridden or almost bedridden for a couple of years. With the help of her sister and the physiotherapist she could just about get downstairs once a week.

Jackie had been a great horsewoman in the past and had a long-standing love affair with John Wayne — only, alas, via the silver screen.

The occupational therapy people fitted her with a chair lift, very similar to a ski-lift, to go up and down the stairs. Jackie could just make it from the bed to the lift on her own, but once

there she enjoyed herself. Often she would spend the morning whizzing up and down the stairs chasing the cat.

'It's the nearest I'll ever get to riding to hounds again,' she said.

Reg Dawkins, my chair-bound patient with an obscure disease, was delighted with the occupational therapists' gadgets and aids.

They gave him a new chair that he could sit up in properly, a new wheelchair that had many advancements on previous ones and, best of all, an electric hoist to get him into the bath.

He insisted that I went to watch his first immersion and ceremoniously we gave his wife, Mary, a crane-driver's certificate. He would swing off his wheelchair into a cradle which lifted him at the press of a button, an arm would then swing down and he could be lowered straight into the bath.

'Bloody marvellous,' said Reg. 'I think this entitles us both to join the Transport and General Workers' Union now.'

Previously Mary had had to wind him up manually on some antiquated contraption to get him into the water.

'The thing that worries me,' I said to Reg, whose lack of mobility had made him put on weight, and who was now hovering around the eighteen stone mark, 'what happens if there is a power cut and you're stuck in the bath?'

'There is only one thing for it,' said Reg, 'I'll get my Mary to light a fire under the bath and then I'll simmer gently until the electricity comes back on.'

CHAPTER 3

Going Off with a Bang

One of the natural wonders of Tadchester was the great annual elver run up the River Tad.

Tiny elvers — transparent baby eels no more than three inches long — swarmed upriver in countless millions every spring, migrating from their birthplace in the mid-Atlantic Sargasso Sea, back to the fresh waters their parents came from.

When the run was on, the town went into a kind of frenzy. Everyone who could, dropped what he or she was doing and ran down to the river with nets, sieves, bowls, buckets — anything with which to scoop up the tiny creatures.

The run was signalled at the mouth of the estuary by the shrieking and wheeling of gulls, and by the appearance of dive-bombing cormorants. This was the sign for the salmon-net fishermen to put away their seine nets and set out their fine-meshed elver nets, to haul catches sometimes weighing hundreds of pounds in a couple of hours or so.

These commercially caught fish would be sold to Pascoes' processing factory at Stowin, who would pack them in ice and send them out all over the country and to the Continent, canning any surplus.

All the way from the Sargasso, the endless streams of elvers had been harried by predatory fish and birds. It was a wonder that any reached the estuary at all, let alone survived the concentrated onslaught of the net fishermen, to carry on upriver into and beyond the town.

Yet there they were, solid silver streams of them, the van-guard now well clear of the commercial nets and swimming straight into the makeshift equipment of the locals in the middle of town. They were scooped out in their thousands and dumped into buckets to be eaten as delicacies in the Tadchester restaurants, as an annual treat in hundreds of ordinary homes, and gulped down by the pound in the elver-eating contests held in almost every local pub.

I was standing on Tadchester Bridge, gazing downstream at the frantic activity, when there was a hooting and a shout from a Land-Rover which had pulled up behind me.

'Jump in, Bob, if you're free. We'll get away from these mad buggers and get our own elvers.'

It was John Denton, the local river bailiff. It was strange to hear a broad Manchester accent from a Tadchester local, but John had been raised in the industrial North and had settled in Tadchester after his army service.

'Fresh air and peace and quiet; that's what I came to

Tadchester for,' he said as I climbed into the Land-Rover. 'There won't be much peace and quiet in this place today.'

John bombed through the traffic and within minutes we were at his cottage a few miles outside the town. He darted down into the cellar, rummaged about and emerged with two enormous fine-meshed nets on the end of long poles.

'I always carry a spare, Bob,' he said, dumping them in the back of the Land-Rover. 'Give us a lift with this bath, will you? There's a good lad.'

On the wall of the cellar hung a large zinc bath. John lifted it down and loaded it with four large buckets.

'Right, then. Grab yourself that pair of wellies in the corner and we're off.'

We raced down to where the river curved in a smooth, incoming bow to form a long and gentle bay. The bank dropped steeply to a flat sand bar four or five feet below.

'This is the best place, Bob,' said John. 'The elvers swing in with the current, almost to the bank. Now let's get the stall set out before they arrive.'

He left the bath just behind us at the top of the bank, tipped in two or three inches of river water, then laid out the buckets on the sand bar in pairs part filled with water and with about ten yards between them.

'When the elvers arrive, Bob, just scoop 'em out, then tip the lot into the buckets. When the buckets are full, climb up the bank and tip the lot into the bath. Then get back down here quick for another go.

'Oh, Rule One with the net: don't slosh it in. Just dip it in smoothly, then a straight sweep downstream into the run.'

'Why the buckets?' I asked. 'Why not just have the bath down here?'

'You ever lifted a tin bath half full of elvers and water up a five-foot bank?' said John. 'You can try it if you like but I'd put your truss on first.'

Ask a silly question...

Ten minutes ticked by and there was no sign of any activity. 'How will we know they're coming?' I asked.

'You'll know,' said John. 'You won't have to be told. Just keep your eyes downstream.'

As I watched, two figures appeared at the end of the bay, carrying nets and buckets just as we were. Was this the sign I was looking for?

'Hey! You two!' shouted John. 'Hop it! Down the town or I'll book you! Go on — bugger off!'

John was an excellent bailiff, but diplomacy had never been his forte. And the pair was obviously not the sign I was looking for.

'What's the problem, John?' I asked. 'Won't there be enough for them as well?'

'Not the point, Bob. Fishing in the town is free by ancient charter. Anyone's welcome to have a go there. But this stretch is ticket water. No ticket, no fishing. Let one get away with it and you'd be trampled to death by half of Tadchester.'

'But they might have tickets.'

'Those two? No chance. Two of the biggest deadlegs in town.

'One of my stockponds was thinned out the other week by a person or persons unknown. Couple of hundred table-sized trout went absent without leave. The person or persons unknown are those two buggers, so my sources tell me. Apart from applying the toe of my wellie, there's not a lot I can do about it now.

'But don't worry. I'm being tipped off in advance the next time they propose to call. And Geoff Emsworth from the Tadchester Arms is going to lend me his guard dog. Hound of the "Bastardvilles" is that one. By the time those two get to court they won't have a leg to stand on, not after that dog's finished with them, anyway.'

The two figures had disappeared. John climbed the bank to be sure they were heading for the road, and made one or two abusive gestures to speed them on their way.

A strange quiet had fallen over the river. Ten minutes passed. Fifteen. Then the water at our feet started to ripple with a silver sheen, and then to boil as dozens of fish cut the surface with their fins and dived down again.

34

From the downstream end of the bay came the raucous cries of gulls. They appeared in a whirling cloud, swooping down again and again onto the water. They were joined by a sudden iridescent flash of colour as a kingfisher shot like a bullet from a branch. And a great grey heron glided down and took up station in the shallows. Within seconds its wicked beak was stabbing down.

'Here they are,' said John. 'Little beauties.'

'What are those fish breaking the surface?'

'Perch, most likely. They hunt in packs, just like wolves. They round up the elvers then dive straight into the middle of them. There'll be trout and chub having a go as well, and perhaps the odd little jack pike. The bigger pike will probably wait until the other fish have had their fill and then pick off some of them while they're digesting their dinner.'

The splashing fish moved past us and the water settled down. Now I could see the massed ranks of tiny silver eels moving steadily past us.

'Right,' said John. 'Eyes down, looking.'

I followed his example and stuck the net in the water, scooping it back downstream in a long, steady sweep. Resistance on the handle increased as the elvers filled the net. A steady lift, and up it came, sagging with a glistening ball of solid silver.

A quick shake and the ball was in the bucket, where it broke up in the water into hundreds of frantic, matchstick-like fish.

'Wonderful,' I said.

'Plenty more where they came from,' called John, shaking his net into one of his own buckets. 'Don't waste time looking at 'em.'

In about fifteen minutes both my buckets were full. As I lurched to the top of the steep bank, I realised the wisdom of leaving the bath where it was. John and I were scooping for an hour, and then the run petered out. For some minutes our nets came up containing just a few stragglers. The gulls had disappeared upstream, pursuing the main run of survivors.

'That's it,' said John. 'For the time being, anyway. There's a break in the run, possibly because the estuary netsmen cut it up, but probably because the tide's begun to turn. There's plenty for what we want, anyway. And there'll be more tonight and tomorrow, if need be.'

Between us, in just over an hour, we must have scooped out about forty pounds of the tiny eels. The bath was alive with their frenetic wriggling. It seemed impossible that such frail and vulnerable creatures could have made their way across the Atlantic in such incredible numbers. But they had done, and had been doing so since before the first man walked the earth.

John and I lurched back to the Land-Rover, lugging the bath between us.

'What are you going to do with all this lot, John?'

'Drop about half of them off at the Tadchester Arms — Geoff's missis makes a lovely elver pie. Then we'll call on some old dears who otherwise might not get any. Then we'll go back and have a fry-up, and what's left we'll split. I'm sure Pam will fancy having a go at some of these.'

We did the rounds, calling first at the back door of the Tadchester Arms, where Geoff Emsworth treated us both to a couple of pints of his best.

'OK, boy. Friends!' Geoff said to the huge, snarling Alsatian which had come up behind him. This was the dog John proposed to borrow to deal with the thefts from his stock pond. I felt sorry for the poachers: 'not a leg to stand on' would be just about right.

Then we called at the houses of eight or ten frail old people to whom John apparently slipped presents of the occasional fish. Their eyes lit up when they saw the elvers. The eels were an annual treat they'd known from childhood, and without John they might have been left out of the town's celebrations.

Back to John's cottage, where he fried some of the elvers and topped two helpings off with an egg apiece. They were really delicious. I was a bit worried about the fact that they were too small to clean, and had to be eaten heads, eyes, innards and all, but John reassured me.

'Nobody in this town has ever died from eating elvers, Bob. At least nobbut the out-and-out gluttons. Oh, and tell Pam the secret is not to over-fry them. If you let them get crispy you've lost half the flavour.'

John drove me back home, a bucket holding about five pounds of elvers sloshing between my knees. Naturally, we had elvers that night.

'Delicious,' said Pam.

'Yummy!' said the kids. 'More, please...'

I just had one helping, including the egg on top. It is possible to have too much of even as good a thing as an elver fry-up. And I could still hear John saying, 'Nobbut the out-and-out gluttons.'

* * *

I saw John the next day. I was fighting off a condition known as Elver Bends, which is a sort of abdominal colic, caused by over-elver consumption.

'Touch of the bends, eh, Bob lad?' said the grinning John. 'A large port and brandy and you'll be as fit as a flea in a couple of hours.'

This was a typical John Denton remedy.

'Eel slaughter,' I replied. 'All those little elvers that will never grow up into eels.'

'Slaughter, nothing,' said John. 'You ought to have been with me when I worked on the Kiltern Estate.'

Five miles to the north of Tadchester lay the Kiltern Estate: 20,000 acres of farm and woodland, several large lakes and a large Elizabethan manor house which even in post-war austerity maintained a massive retinue of servants, maids and grooms.

It was one of the few titled estates that flourished economically. There was money to maintain this grandiose building and there was money for anything young Lord Kiltern desired.

The source of the money was nothing very romantic. It wasn't oil or inherited wealth: it was simply gravel. Many acres of the estate contained highest quality gravel under a very thin layer of top soil and Kiltern gravel appeared on most of the main roads and motorways throughout the country.

The holes left by the excavation of gravel had formed large lakes, some of which had been taken over for sailing, water-skiing and fishing. It was said that one of the qualifications to be taken on the Kiltern staff was to be web-footed.

The estate was run not by the young Lord Kiltern, who would not let anything distract him from his main hobby, but by a board of trustees. They gave Lord Kiltern such a large monthly allowance that it was difficult for him to spend it all however extravagant he tried to be.

His father had been killed during the war and his mother, tottering and prematurely aged, had gone to live in Switzerland in a sort of alcoholics' commune.

Lord Kiltern was able to do exactly as he wanted, and he did. He experimented with every facet of life: drink, drugs, girls, boys, men, women, the lot. In his twenties he travelled around the world as a sort of well-breeched layabout with a retinue of hangers-on who, numerous though they were, still never made any real dent in the Kiltern fortunes.

Having done all that there was to do, and having done it two or three times, at the ripe old age of twenty-eight Lord Kiltern came back to his ancestral home to settle down and indulge in his only real love, shooting.

Some men take great pride in their proficiency as marksmen and enter shooting competitions such as Bisley. Others' prowess is in the number of clay pigeons they can shoot in a certain period of time.

But Lord Kiltern's motivation was much simpler: he was a killer.

He shot everything that moved.

Vast numbers of birds — pheasants and ducks — were raised on his estate, and he would even go and shoot turkeys and geese when they were needed for the table. His appetite for slaughter was insatiable. Everything shootable was shot.

He went up to Scotland for the Glorious Twelfth for his grouse and part of the year was always spent stag-shooting in the Highlands.

Until he was thirty he still made the odd trip to go off and shoot wild boar or big game, but his health, because of the ravages he had imposed upon himself, declined and he became less and less mobile. He had a gun in his hand all day and when he wasn't firing it he was oiling it or cleaning it, and most of his days, when he wasn't out killing something, were spent in his gun room.

Lord Kiltern tried to shoot something every day. When he had run out of all legitimate game he would wander round the stables attached to the great house firing at rats and causing considerable damage to stable doors.

The area round the estate gradually became denuded of wild-life and there had to be imports of even such fast breeders as rabbits. The surviving animals on his estate had adapted to their environment. There was one huge rabbit burrow about a half a mile from the main house, and it had so many holes that there was always a way for the rabbits to escape. It was a thorn in Lord Kiltern's side.

He was determined to beat this impregnable rabbit warren and planned an attack with as much attention to detail as if it were the D-Day landing.

An organ in the main chapel of Kiltern Manor was dis-mantled and the larger organ pipes were taken out to the rabbit warren and stuck in the various rabbit holes. Keepers, dogs, and beaters were organised and with the stage set, the organ pipes sticking out of the ground like the guns of a great battleship, Lord Kiltern was pushed to the scene of the action in a wheel-chair. His abuse of drink and drugs had progressively damaged his kidneys and he had become no longer fit enough to get round the estate under his own steam.

Thirty or so men and dogs were put to work to blockade all the holes not covered by organ pipes, servants were posted by each pipe and ferrets were sent down. The excitement was tremendous. As the pipes were long the servant by each pipe would hear when a rabbit was about to exit. There would be a shout of 'High G, m'Lord,' and a rabbit would pop out of the end of the appropriate organ pipe to be blasted into extinction. 'Low C, m'lord!' and bang! — another rabbit bit the dust. Nearly forty rabbits were collected that day, most of them too smashed to be edible, and the young Lord Kiltern finished up beaming with satisfaction.

His health worsened. He was confined permanently to a chair and his shooting — now from the dining-room window — became more and more bizarre.

On the day he died of renal failure at the age of thirty-five, he had ordered the roof of his conservatory to be removed. Nearly every worker on his estate was dragooned into attempting to drive pheasants across this empty air space. It often meant carrying a pheasant to just outside the door and throwing it up into the air, while the noble lord blazed away. He had a tremendous bag and died, as they say, with a smile on his face.

'I expect that's what they mean when they say "He went in a blaze of glory,"' said John Denton.

'We won't see the likes of him again, thank God.'

'I'll stick to my elvers.'

CHAPTER 4

Normally Abnormal

When I first came to Tadchester I was amazed at the variety of conditions that patients produced: conditions that I had never dreamt possible, things that I hadn't been taught about at medical school.

I was always rushing off to my partners with tales of new and incredible discoveries such as the Irish girl who thought she could suffocate an unwanted pregnancy by sticking Elastoplast over her navel, and the man who took his cat's worming pills by mistake for his arthritis and found they improved him. It was almost as if the normal was the abnormal.

My successes weren't in brilliant diagnoses, but in catching diseases in time and referring them to expert help. And a lot of my work consisted of seeing people through difficult situations.

It was just as important to see that Mrs Jones got going under her own steam again after the loss of her husband, as it was to prove that Mrs Smith had sub-acute bacterial endocarditis.

I considered my greatest medical achievement was the handling of the case of seven-year-old John Turpin.

Before he reached me, he had been seen by all my four partners, two paediatric specialists, one child psychiatrist and

had nearly driven them and his father and mother literally and metaphorically potty.

Johnny Turpin wouldn't open his bowels. He would scream whenever he was taken to the toilet, and every seven days had to be knelt on while suppositories were inserted.

His bowels dominated the whole household. Other members of the family were all nervous wrecks. Both his mother and father were on tranquillisers. His elder brother and sister were very edgy and their schoolwork was falling off.

Medical investigation excluded any organic causes for Johnny's trouble. It was a battle of wills.

It was always a fight to get any medicine down Johnny. He

would never go to the toilet, but would either have an accident in his pants or in the bath. He could honestly be called a 'little stinker'.

His parents were neat, tidy and fastidious. His father had a senior position at the town hall. Their house was spotless and this little smelly son of theirs was really upsetting them.

I'd heard about Johnny from my partners, all of whom had reached an impasse in their attempts to treat him.

He was sent away to a special boarding school where they dealt with this type of problem, but he refused to eat and drink and screamed all the time until they brought him home, just as bad as ever.

The Turpin parents came to my surgery one day, extremely apologetic and in no way wanting to criticise my partners for all the kind work they and the specialists had done. But they were in despair. Was there anything I could suggest?

I told them that Johnny had been seen by the best opinions available, and I didn't know of anything that I could offer. As a last resort, however, I was very happy to see him, and we could take it from there.

They brought in the glowering little Turpin the next day.

He sat on a chair looking at me suspiciously. He had been through all this before. I was one of that group who, given a chance, would stick a finger up his bottom and cause him to scream the place down.

I tried to ask him about why he didn't go to the toilet but made no progress: there was no communication at all. Suddenly I had an idea.

'Johnny,' I said.

He hung his head.

'Johnny,' I said, 'look at me.'

Reluctantly he looked at me.

I said, 'If, for four weeks, you go to the toilet regularly, without a fuss, I will give you five shillings which you can spend on anything you like.'

'Oh, Doctor, you shouldn't,' said Mrs Turpin.

'No, that's all right,' I said. 'It's between Johnny and myself.'

'All right, Johnny?'

There was a half nod of assent.

I made a note on his record card: 'Give five shillings if opens bowels regularly for four weeks.'

Four weeks later he came back. Instead of having to be dragged into the surgery, Johnny came bounding in, followed by a flushed and beaming mother.

'How's he done?' I asked.

'Marvellous, Doctor. We've had no trouble at all. It's been like a miracle.'

I put my hand in my pocket — no change. Generosity had to be the order of the day.

'Here you are, Johnny,' I said. 'Ten shillings — well done.'

His face lit up.

'Five shillings to go in the post office and five shillings to be spent on sweets.'

'Oh, Doctor,' said Mrs Turpin, 'you are marvellous.'

A month later he came in beaming again and collected another ten shillings which his mother insisted on paying back. For my trouble she left a bottle of five-star brandy with a note that I was the best doctor in the world.

They must have worked out a system of rewards of their own, as I never saw Johnny again. I only hope I hadn't completely corrupted him.

Occasionally from then on, new patients came to register with me, saying that Mr and Mrs Turpin had recommended me.

Thus are reputations made.

* * *

I imagine that my patients and their idiosyncrasies were unique, but expect that most general practices could provide a cross-section of the sort of people I had to deal with.

After some years nothing really surprised me.

Charlie Hutt was actually one of Henry's patients. I used to see him coming to the surgery in his little three-wheeler. He lived on his own in a terraced house near the surgery.

46

He'd been a forester in the past and was under retiring age but not working, obviously crippled by either arthritis or some accident. He went everywhere with elbow crutches, limping along, swinging one leg after the other, grimacing with pain.

He always wore a brown leather bomber jacket and brown corduroy trousers. He had shoulder-length untidy hair, thinning in the front and was one of the Tadchester characters. He was not a pub man but would be seen on the quay resting on his crutches, yarning with the fishermen, or in the pannier market, chatting. He was a great talker, and would always pass the time of day with me.

I don't know what he did apart from look after himself and go out chatting. I admired his courage and the way he struggled along with his elbow crutches.

They say everybody has a double and one day I saw Charlie's.

About ten miles outside Tadchester the Forestry Commission had some estates of pines. My friend Eric was delivering a television set to a remote farm near there and as I had the afternoon off I went along for the ride.

Driving along the roadway through the pines we came across the exact double of Charlie Hutt. A man with shoulder-length hair, thinning at the front, brown bomber jacket, brown corduroy trousers, striding along with a chain-link saw in one hand and a log of wood over his shoulder.

I don't ever remember seeing two people looking so absolutely alike, and wondered if Charlie had had a twin.

The next day in surgery I was telling Henry about this amazing Charlie lookalike.

'Good Lord, Bob lad,' guffawed Henry. 'That was Charlie.'

'But,' I said, 'he was walking upright carrying a chain-link saw. He looked perfectly fit.'

'I know,' said Henry. 'About seven years ago Charlie's missus left him. He immediately started to walk with a limp and decided that he was going to use a pair of arm crutches. We've had him X-rayed, examined him, turned him upsidedown — there's nothing wrong with him.

'From time to time he gets fed up with being an invalid and

goes off and spends a day doing forestry work. They pay him a few quid; he's a very good tree surgeon.

'He's just made up his mind he wants to walk with crutches and there's nothing we can do to stop him. But don't you tell him you've seen him in the forests — he'll put a gipsy's curse on you.'

I didn't tell Charlie. A gipsy's curse was about all I needed.

Charlie was just one of a large group of patients who confirmed that, for Tadchester anyway, it was the abnormal that was really the normal.

* * *

Ray Short was our plumber. He had first come on the scene as a plumber's apprentice with one of the established firms in the town. We were so impressed with his tidiness, general application and modest bills that when he set up on his own, we signed up with him as our regular. He was a neat, compact, rather nervous little chap and his slender little wife, Joan, was a patient of mine. Neither of them was above 5 foot 6 inches.

Some people are more married than others, and Ray and Joan were much more than most. Their family was their life.

In days when most people had two children, Ray and Joan earnestly planned four at the right intervals and every eighteen months along came a child, right on time with no complications or fuss. Joan was a marvellous mum to her bonny children, whom she clothed in hand-knitted jumpers and tights. To complete the planning, six weeks after the birth of the fourth baby Joan was sterilised.

Ray was an industrious fellow. Their home, a large detached house near the park, was always immaculate and the garden looked as if it had come straight from a seed catalogue. They were very busy being man, wife and family, devoting all their time to the home and garden, budgie, cat, two dogs and a rabbit. Joan was a member of the Women's Institute and the young mothers' club, and they were as solid and respectable and pleasant as you could wish: a couple who were the absolute pillar not only of any community but of society itself.

All seemed to be well with them. The children came to the surgery for their various injections and checks but they were rarely ill. They were extremely well looked after. When the youngest came for his measles injection I did notice that Joan was rather plumper than I had remembered.

The next time I saw her she was a bit plumper still. I made some comment and the normally unflappable, motherly Joan was very tense and taut.

'Oh, we've got a lot of worry on, Doctor,' she said, 'what with me taking O-levels at night school and things being so hard in the plumbing business.' A large firm of plumbers had recently set up in the town and were in fierce competition with Ray's one-man outfit.

When I passed Ray in the street or he came down to do a job, he looked much more serious, almost as if life was getting too much for him. He had always been versatile and although ostensibly he was our plumber, he would clean gutters for us, put back tiles, put in window cords and even new windows. His bills, which had always been too modest for the amount of work he did, now went the other way and were much more than anyone else's. Instead of his increased prices helping settle his financial condition, they aggravated it because people turned to the less expensive, though not as conscientious, larger firms.

Things got worse and worse until the cold winter of 1963, which was every plumber's dream. I think that every pipe in the town that could burst, did. The plumbers were working round the clock, and Ray was able to stabilise his economic situation.

The lines began to disappear from his face, and Joan looked happier. But still she got progressively fatter. The next time she came in with one of the children — apart from pregnancies she never came about her own health — I felt I had to intercede. She really was getting extremely gross now and as her clothes did not keep up with her weight she was beginning to bulge out of everything.

'Joan,' I said, 'we must do something about your weight.'

She replied, as most over-weight people do, 'Oh, I hardly ever eat anything, Doctor. It must be my glands.'

The next time Ray came round, I mentioned it to him.

'She eats very little, Doctor,' said the defensive Ray. 'I know she does.'

Joan, like Topsy, whatever she said about her diet, growed and growed and growed. Her blood pressure began to go up and she was a good eighteen and a half stone. I remembered that after her first baby she was only six and a half stone.

I screened her with various blood tests but apart from a fairly high blood sugar level, everything seemed normal. I sent her off to Winchcombe to John Bowler who investigated her thoroughly and could find no organic cause for her steadily increasing weight.

I took Ray to task again about how much she ate. He swore that she ate very little. 'Honest, Doctor, there's never very much food in the house. Joan doesn't believe in stocking up.'

I gave her diet sheets and slimming pills but, in spite of all my efforts, she continued to grow.

I discussed it with my partners, but none of them could give me any ideas. I suggested that we admit Joan to Tadchester Hospital to keep an eye on her diet but she refused because of the children.

She really was a sight now, fat and bloated. Her weight, apart from making her uncomfortable, was causing her a great deal of distress.

'Oh, Doctor, I do wish I could lose weight,' she said. 'Isn't there something I could take?'

She made a sorry picture, sobbing, her great big fat arms shaking and tears running down her cheeks.

'I just don't know what to do, Joan,' I said, 'unless we wire your jaw, which I don't think is practical. Let's have a look at your eating list.'

What I found helpful for people trying to lose weight was to make them write down a list of everything that went into their mouth during the day. The fact that they had to write everything down was often good enough to knock off as much as a couple of stone. They had to think before they ate.

As Joan opened her handbag the contents tipped out.

Amongst the lipsticks, powder compact and bus tickets was an envelope of white powder that spilled all over the floor.

'What's this?' I said to Joan.

She had been crying before. She now became completely hysterical. She sat rocking on the chair, arms over her face, crying 'Oh, you've found me out! You've found me out! Doctor, I'm an addict.'

There was very little addiction of any sort in Tadchester and the only people I could think of were the cider addicts who used to congregate near the river bank. I had read in the papers of packets of heroin and cocaine and stuff, but surely Joan would be the last person to be associated with anything like that?

'Addicted to what?' I asked.

Joan through her muffled sobs, said, 'Icing sugar.'

'What do you mean, icing sugar?' I said.

'I eat a pound of icing sugar each day,' she sobbed, 'and I can't stop.'

'I don't believe you.'

'Yes, I do, Doctor. Please believe me. When we had all the worries about money and my exams, I got into the habit of taking a pinch of icing sugar. It wasn't very expensive and I took more and more and now I can't do without it. I keep on having a dab or a spoonful and I'm getting fatter and fatter and there's nothing I can do about it. Please don't stop me.'

'Joan,' I said, 'I'm writing straight to the *Guinness Book of Records*. You must be the first person in history ever to be addicted to icing sugar. You silly girl, why didn't you come and talk to me before? We could have helped you. There's not going to be any trouble getting you off.'

'I felt so ashamed, Doctor,' she said, 'and I always thought that next week I would be able to give it up, but then next week would come and there'd be some child's birthday and I'd be asked to bake a cake and there'd be some reason for buying icing sugar and now I order eight pounds a week — one pound for cooking and seven pounds for myself.'

'Your troubles are now over, Joan,' I said. 'Now you've told me, we can do something about it. In a few weeks this will all be

a thing of the past. We'll soon have you back to eight stone.'

But I was wrong. When Joan said that she was addicted, she meant it. She had all the problems of withdrawal that people have from the serious addictive drugs. We were at least six months with some psychiatric help getting her off the sugar and it was a year and a half before she got under ten stone. None of Joan's children ever had cakes iced. She just couldn't risk having any in the house.

A few days after Joan's confession I went into Ron Dickinson's surgery. He was holding up an X-ray, looking at it pensively with a fountain pen stuck in his mouth.

'What's the matter, Ron?' I said. 'Have you taken to smoking fountain pens now?'

'Oh, no,' said Ron, 'I'm addicted to them. I eat them all the time.'

'A fortnight ago, Ron,' I said, 'I wouldn't have listened to you, but I completely believe you now. I think I'll have to start flicking pencils in your ears as an antidote.'

*   *   *

Mr and Mrs Rollinson were well into their seventies when I first started to look after them. They had been publicans in London most of their lives and had moved down to Tadchester to run a little mixed groceries shop near the bridge. This they did until their retirement when they moved into a semi-detached house off Park Lane. Long marriages are often endured through love or necessity, or through people enjoying arguing and finding that their partner was the most able arguer they had ever met. But the Rollinsons didn't seem to have anything to keep the marriage going, other than the habit that they had always been together and had always worked together.

They lived their lives in mutual hostility. I, as a common factor, was constantly wooed to take one side or the other and had to keep as neutral as possible. They had a couple of children who lived in London, but they never came to see them.

Mr Rollinson spent his time pottering round his greenhouse and would produce tomatoes for me as a bribe, whereas Mrs Rollinson would never let me go without producing a white and sickly toffee from a huge seven-pound jar.

'Can't go without your sweet, Doctor,' she used to say.

I used to hate it. I would pop it in my mouth and start chewing before I left the house. They were so sticky that you couldn't spit them out afterwards and I had to accept that I was going to have a rotten sticky mouth for the rest of the afternoon.

Both the Rollinsons were seriously convinced that Mr Rollinson was suffering from a brain condition. He was always asking for something for his arthritis. I examined all his joints which, for his age, were very mobile and it was some months before I began to realise that what he was really bothered about was that he thought he had arthritis of the brain.

I fobbed him off with some liquid paraffin. 'It oils all the sticky parts,' I said. He seemed content with this and appeared to improve. I thought arthritis of the brain was quite a good condition to have and added it to my armoury of questions for awkward customers.

If somebody sat down and gave me forty symptoms I would look him straight in the eye and ask 'Do you think you've got arthritis of the brain?' If he said yes I would assume that most of his troubles were psychosomatic.

When I first came into general practice my punch-line when people were going on with innumerable symptoms was to ask 'Do you get pain in the back of the neck when you pass water?'

Having done this for some years and been rather pleased with myself about this clever phrase, I went to a post-graduate course where they described a syndrome called the sub-clavian steal syndrome which meant that if you whirled your arm round it resulted in losing your sight in one eye. So perhaps people did get pain in the back of the neck when they passed water.

Mrs Rollinson had all sorts of bladder troubles, and eventually lost her bladder tone which meant she couldn't pass water.

There was no obstruction but her stomach swelled and she could only pass water in dribbles.

I sent her to hospital for investigations. Calling round to see her soon after she had been discharged, I found her sitting grumpily in a chair, a rug over her knees.

'Fine mess you've got me into, Doctor,' she said, 'sending me to the hospital.'

'Well, Mrs Rollinson,' I said, 'you're looking much better and we had to do something, You couldn't pass your water.'

'Guess what they did to me.'

'I've no idea,' I said.

She said, 'They stuck a cafeteria into me and I've got to keep it stuck in me for the rest of my life.' I nearly exploded with laughing. Lifting the blanket I could see an in-dwelling catheter attached to a collecting bag on her knees.

I thought it was probably some sort of neutral justice that if a man was stuck with arthritis of the brain, he should be married to a woman who sported an in-dwelling cafeteria.

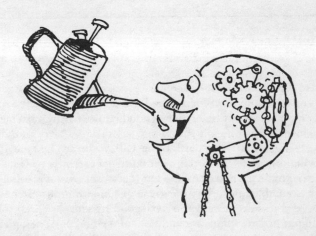

CHAPTER 5

Holidays with the Family

I had been a bachelor when I first arrived in Tadchester, survived the ambitions of several local ladies, and married my wife Pam after meeting her when holidaying with my mother in Bournemouth.

After nine years in a flat Up-the-Hill, we built a house overlooking the estuary. Thinking our family of two boys was all we were going to have, we had got our rooms worked out precisely. Jane, our daughter, was born exactly nine months after we moved. I'm sure there was a very good reason.

In our original plans we had not counted on nurseries, girls' bedrooms, etc. and the tiny study and TV room had to be knocked together to remedy this deficit. The builder said we were the only people he had ever known who started knocking walls down as soon as the house had been put up.

The birth of Jane coincided with the death of Pam's mother, 'Bill'. Pam and her mother had been extremely close but Pam was so occupied with the new baby that frankly she just had not the time to grieve. It was one of those strange balances of nature which can do so much to heal the wounds of tragedy.

But one of the disadvantages of general practice is that the sheer physical demand of the working hours means that the

amount of time you spend with your family, particularly your children, is limited. As I begin to tot up the years, looking back on the things that have given me the greatest pleasure, I think probably the happiest moments of my life have occurred on travels with the family.

It was impossible to have holidays at home, even though we

lived in a delightful rural area near the sea. If I was at home gardening, the fact that my car was outside the house would encourage people to knock at the door with, 'I know you are off duty, Doctor, but . . .'; even a trip to the beach usually resulted in a queue of people waiting to see me for unofficial and alfresco consultations. So when holidays came round we had to get up and travel somewhere.

All five of us reacted differently to the rigours of travelling. The drug companies which sell travel-sickness preparations have always done well out of us. Pam and Jane take one tablet; Paul, my younger son, has at least two, and Trevor none at all. I need a measure of brandy or whisky to wash down a tablet, providing that I have remembered to take it before I've swallowed the supporting fluid.

Pam is patient, long-suffering and non-complaining. A polite request for the car window to be opened slightly means that the combination of my clouds of tobacco smoke, dust and undulations of the road are too much for her, that she is feeling sick, that she wishes she were dead and would rather have stayed at home anyway.

Trevor is unperturbed by travel; in fact, he is unperturbed by anything. He uses bread as a tranquilliser, following each meal with a few thick slices, and at home slips off to the bread bin every fifteen minutes in between meals. I did, on one journey, find him chewing a tyre-pressure gauge, but put it down to withdrawal symptoms as he had been without bread for two hours.

If Trevor is mentioned in the *Guinness Book of Records* for his bread consumption, Paul must rank as the worst traveller of all time. Once, in a rowing boat on Lake Geneva, on a calm, sunny day, he felt sea-sick before we had left the shore. He distinguished himself on that particular holiday by vomiting all the way from Calais to the Italian Riviera and back.

Although we remembered the magnificent scenery, the Alps and the Dura Mountains, he claimed to be more familiar with the bottom of Continental lavatory basins than anyone else of the same age and weight.

On one occasion, crossing on a new and short-lived route to the Continent — Torquay to Cherbourg — on a boat without stabilisers, I thought we were going to lose him.

Everyone on the boat was sick, standing three-deep at the rail, including two hundred Swedish students, all dressed in their Sunday best on a day trip. It was easy to see what you had had for breakfast because the next person was wearing it.

Pam and I were so ill that we could give Paul only the minimum attention. He lay curled up, semi-conscious, under some seats on a pile of newspapers. On disembarking we carried him to the car and — although this was officially a camping holiday — rushed to book in at the nearest (very expensive) hotel to get him safely into bed.

As a small boy Paul always looked desperately ill even when he was well. He was so thin that we considered he might have a career modelling for famine relief posters. This time he looked worse than usual. It was a tremendous relief to get him into bed and see his small pale face lying peacefully on a huge pillow. I popped back half an hour later to see him stirring. 'Paul,' I said, 'is there anything I can get you: Vichy water, lemon squash?'

To my utter amazement for one so young, his feeble voice answered, 'Yes. I would like a sirloin steak, rare, with chips and a tossed salad.'

This was our Paul all over. Although he goes down quicker than anyone I know, there's no doubt that he gets up even faster. He has sometimes been so dehydrated by travel sickness that if he had been a patient I would have sent him to hospital. But put Paul to bed, give him twenty minutes after he has stopped being sick and he is up, downing a plate of egg and chips before shooting off to play football.

His ability to eat in unusual circumstances could be due to pre-natal influences by his brother. At three o'clock one April morning I was rushing Pam by car, in early labour with Paul, to the maternity hospital. Trevor, aged three, and lying supposedly asleep on the back seat, suddenly piped up, 'We haven't had swede for lunch lately, have we?'

Jane, much like her mother, is the gentlest of the three children: a sweet, tender little soul. She is highly intelligent as well as being painstaking and methodical. She is a fair traveller and takes her medication reluctantly.

I, as the last-mentioned traveller of the family, am the leader, the organiser, and the only smoking member. As I get older I get fatter and balder and more addicted to my pipe. I am one of the few people who smoke a pipe in bed before breakfast and have been known to nip down in the night for a puff. I have an excellent reason for smoking a pipe: I can't afford cigars.

My life has been so permeated with smoke that my partners reckoned they could smell me coming even if I weren't smoking.

A long train journey with Ron Dickinson after a hospital reunion in London, resulted in his wife forbidding him ever to travel with me again. She said not only did his clothes smell of pipe smoke for weeks, but the whole of the wardrobe had become contaminated.

The family has always travelled in rather old and suspect cars. I begrudge spending money on cars and can never understand why they fall to pieces. We take enough food and clothes for a month, irrespective of the fact that our holiday may only be for a week. There are polythene bags hanging out of windows, chairs and tables strapped untidily to the roof rack; every available inch around the car passengers is crammed with shoes, packets of cornflakes, tennis rackets etc.

We would make ideal smugglers. No customs official would ever dream of interfering with the turmoil of our car luggage. From our outward appearance, even if we were illegally trafficking, we were obviously not making a profit out of it.

* * *

River holidays had been a success in the past, so one year we booked a barge holiday on the River Severn and the adjoining canal system.

We travelled by car to the Severn, to a beautiful marina filled with gleaming, modern boats. In previous years we always seemed to have a dirty old boat: perhaps our luck was in this time. There were some 150 boats in the marina. They really were superb, being beautifully equipped and more like floating bungalows than boats.

Our boat turned out to be one of a group of grimy barges moored some 100 yards away from the main huddle. (Perhaps if they were closer they would have contaminated the others.) Our luck hadn't changed. And, as it turned out, we were paying more for ours than for one of the brand new models.

The boat was a 50 foot long, six-berth steel barge. It was the best equipped boat we had ever had, with electric light, hot water, flush toilet, shower, gas stove, fridge and convector heater.

It was also the dirtiest boat we had ever had. No attempt had been made to clear accumulated mud and debris either inside or outside.

We tested the various equipment and found that the water heater didn't work, the fridge didn't work, and we didn't know how to light the convector heater. From time to time we engaged the attention of men in smart nylon overalls. Whoever we contacted seemed to be involved in something else and promised to get his mate who specialised in our particular problem, in five minutes.

Nobody took our inventory, and anyway we couldn't find one. We did note that we had no mop, deck scrubbers, mooring stakes, windlasses for opening locks, mallet, or engine oil. Each time we asked one of our marina staff for some particular missing item, he would soon manage to produce it. It was only later I noticed they were pinching them from other boats.

We had ordered a television set and eventually a battered one materialised. The man who brought it cheerfully said, 'If you can't get it to work, we will give you your money back.'

Having stowed our luggage we sat waiting for someone to come and authorise the hire. In the meantime, relays of men, each saying it wasn't really his job, managed to get our water heater going, our fridge in working order, and instruct us how to use the convector heater.

We were due to take over the boat at 4 p.m. It was 6.45 p.m. before the boat proprietor arrived to conduct the business side. There were one or two surprises, including an extortionate charge for parking our car for the week.

One of the engineers showed us the various working parts of the boat, turned the engine on and we cast off. He opened the throttle handle and it came away in his hand.

'That's definitely not good,' he said.

The boat could do eight or nine knots, it was steel-hulled and weighed a few tons and if not under reasonable control could do a great deal of damage. The engineer screwed the throttle handle back on, leapt off the boat, and we were away.

We had planned to cruise from the Severn to the Avon, go up to Stratford and, hopefully, go to the theatre. We discovered that the lock gates into the Avon were under repair and closed to traffic. So we headed upstream to the canals that would lead us into the Midlands.

We cruised for about an hour then moored out in the country by a field. Although it was a six-berth boat, there was only seating for three round the table, so I stood up having my dinner at the sink and Paul sat on the steps leading up to the front of the boat, with his dinner on his knees. The disadvantage of sitting on the steps was that they were next to the convector heater — which really was hot. Although Paul thoroughly enjoyed his meal he found that he had burnt a hole in his jeans.

Going up the Severn I appreciated for the first time some of the things that Captain Scott put up with. In my exposed position as helmsman I bore the full brunt of the wind, rain, hail and icy cold. It was no comfort to know that I was paying through the nose for the experience.

On the second day, in the teeth of a driving gale, we reached our first lock, on the Severn just south of Worcester. Manoeuvring the boat in the lock I put it astern with full throttle to bring it to a halt.

The throttle handle came off in my hand and several tons of steel barge were bearing down on the lock gates with nothing to stop them. As calmly as I could, I knelt down by the instrument

post and tried to fit the throttle handle into its socket to reduce the revolutions. Thankfully, with one son holding it in place, I was able to bring the boat to a stop.

The lockkeeper had various screwdrivers but none of them fitted the handle. Eventually I managed to effect some sort of repair by using an assortment of medical instruments. (I had thrown my medical instrument case in, as I usually run into surgical difficulties on holiday.) These instruments took a greater beating on the barge than they had during my previous ten years in medicine. My midwifery scissors were used (to their detriment) when we found that the only tin opener provided on board didn't work.

Next day, we reached Stourport for lunch and thought we had come to Blackpool by mistake. It seemed a mass of crowds, fairgrounds, and fish-and-chip shops. We had been told to keep our water tank topped up, with the attendant vaguely pointing to the white caps on the top of the cabin which, as old boat hands, we knew were the covers to the water tank. We successfully started a stream of water going through the hole on the top of the boat. Fortunately Jane was reading below and, hearing a splashing noise, informed us that we were putting water through the bathroom ventilator.

Eventually we were away and up the Worcester and Stafford Canal.

We crept through the dismal industrial area of Kidderminster, past derelict factories, sewage works, and one lock right in the middle of the town with traffic pouring over our heads. Then we were in the country again and found a delightful mooring spot close to a lock pub at Wolverley.

One day the family got back to the boat to find Trevor holding it to the bank by the two ropes. He had got so caught up in a book he was reading in the cabin that he had not heard a party of youths come along, pinch the aluminium mooring pegs, coil the ropes on the barge and push it into mid stream.

Almost as if from a storybook we found a real live blacksmith with a forge by the towpath. He fashioned us some iron mooring pegs, one of which seemed to weigh about three quarters of a ton.

After a few more adventures, we found ourselves back at the mooring on the Severn.

We'd enjoyed the holiday. It had been nice to be cruising along knowing there was a joint roasting in the oven and that the cabin would be warm and there would be a bottle of wine waiting. You have got to get wet and cold to really appreciate warmth and dryness. To manage the boat we all had to leap about and in spite of ourselves we had become quite fit.

We needed the fitness when we got to the marina car park — ours was the only car which wouldn't start.

CHAPTER 6

Rewarding Years

I was called urgently one day to help Jack Hart with a male patient who had collapsed just outside the surgery. In spite of all our resuscitation attempts, he died.

'He was sitting in my surgery half an hour ago, talking to me,' said Jack, 'I'll have to inform the coroner.' (All deaths have to be reported to a coroner if the deceased has not seen a doctor in the previous two weeks.)

'Why, Jack?' I asked. 'You've only just seen him.'

Jack looked a bit sheepish. 'He's not a patient of ours,' he said. 'I've just done a life insurance examination on him.'

'And how did you grade him?'

'An A1 first-class risk.'

I always avoided being pinned down to a forecast on how long people are likely to survive in any particular circumstances. Too often I have been proved wrong. I've comforted families whose elderly relatives I thought would pass away during the night, to be confounded by them being hale and hearty five years later.

New cures arrive almost every day which can completely change the outlook on certain diseases. When penicillin was discovered, five diseases which were considered incurable, straightaway became curable and manageable. This was apart from all the lesser benefits that penicillin and similar drugs brought to the treatment of other diseases.

I also believe that if you tell a man that he only has a certain time to live then, whatever else you do, you reduce the time he has to spend with us.

Two couples defied all the odds.

Commander Hugh Dunlop and his wife Erica were both ex-navy people. Commander Dunlop was 6 foot 4 inches, seventeen stone and practically housebound by a painful arthritic hip. Erica, a pert, very upper crust ex-Wren, was charming, smiling, very attractive and in her early sixties.

The Dunlops lived in a little cottage at the end of a small mews just off the front at Sanford-on-Sea, or rather this was where Hugh held court.

The cottage was extremely tiny and its living room crammed with antiques. It had a kitchen and bathroom at the back and a winding staircase leading to bedrooms upstairs.

The small front garden was packed with flowers and there were roses over the door: the archetypal dream cottage. It was the focal point of local activity, with a constant stream of visitors coming and going.

The Dunlops were the perfect hosts, always charming, although Hugh was physically very limited. Erica looked well but was, in fact, far from it.

I had been visiting them for some years, treating Hugh's arthritis, when Erica asked if I would mind having a look at her. She had, to my knowledge, never had any medical attention before.

We climbed the tiny spiral staircase to the bedroom. On examining Erica I found that she had a widespread cancer. My heart sank.

'How long have you had these lumps, Erica?' I asked.

'Oh, about two years,' she replied. 'I didn't like to bother anybody.'

Erica had to have a mutilating and debilitating operation, and then fight a constant battle against the invading disease.

I would have said that she had about six months to live.

However, she went on leading a normal life to the extent that she ran her household, did her own shopping, did not reduce the amount she entertained and was able to attend local dinners and cocktail parties.

She had to have repeated courses of radiotherapy and various courses of drugs. Although at times she must have felt absolutely awful, particularly when she was on some of the more toxic drug treatments, she never complained. She never ever asked what was wrong with her, she appeared to accept that she had some sort of inflammatory condition — so there was no need to dwell on the reality of her condition. I think she knew the truth but had managed to shut it out.

Erica's disease, though not cured, was contained. She lived a normal life to its full span — and none of us can hope for much more than that.

Hugh knew absolutely everything and everybody. Whatever subject you brought up, he was better informed than you. He made it his business to keep in touch with all the important people he knew and he knew so many: lords, ladies, politicians, generals, admirals. Hardly a day went by without someone calling at the cottage. There were army staff cars, Rolls-Royces, battered sports cars, even bicycles, parked outside. There was always something going on.

Hugh had been injured in the Norwegian expedition during the war, and had been decorated by both British and Norwegian Governments. Manning a Bofors gun on the quay as they left Norway chased by the Germans, with too long an exposure to the flashes, had left him with some weakening of his sight. Although he could hear quite well, his eyes were such that he couldn't read. He was unable to watch television, but he wouldn't have had time anyway. Once when he was admitted to hospital he had twice as many visitors as the person next to him in popularity. He also had the largest fund of dirty stories I have ever known.

For all his cheerfulness and bluff naval manner, Hugh was in considerable pain. I never knew how he got up and down the stairs from his bedroom to the living room: it must have been on his hands and knees.

His hip got progressively worse and it was obvious that he should have something surgical done. I impressed on him that he must see an orthopaedic surgeon.

'Thank you, old boy,' said Hugh. 'We'll think it over and let you know.'

By my next visit — and the visits were usually more social than medical (I could hardly ever get away without a glass of whisky from a cut glass decanter) — Hugh and Erica had thought it over. Said Hugh, 'We have decided to have Chaplin operate on my hips, old boy. All my friends say he is the best.'

'That will cost you the earth,' I said. 'Chaplin is the most famous hip surgeon in England.'

'Oh, I know,' said Hugh. 'We obviously can't afford his fees so I will go and see him privately at first — when he visits the south of England — and then I'll go up and have it done in one of his National Health beds at Wrightington, near Wigan.'

'Hugh,' I said, 'everybody wants him. It's like saying I would like to have the Queen's physician for my bronchitis.'

'Look here, old boy,' said Hugh, 'this is what we want. Please organise it.'

This was how Hugh always operated. I sat down and wrote a long letter to Chaplin who I knew had a waiting list of private patients for two years and National Health for three years. I wrote explaining how ill both Hugh and Erica were, and put forward — tentatively and apologetically — Hugh's proposition.

To my surprise, an appointment came in two weeks for Hugh to be seen at Midhurst in Sussex. Six weeks later he was in Wrightington having his operation under the National Health Service. The logistics of getting him up to Wrightington and back were incredible, but friends stood the costs of all train journeys and went to great lengths to organise cars in between. Hugh was back in two months, having done what he set out to do. He'd had his hip operation by the best man in the land and there was one more story for his repertoire. Of course, by then he was an authority on Chaplin and had another celebrated name to add to his list.

A couple of years went by and Hugh's other hip started to give trouble.

'I'm thinking of getting in touch with Chaplin again,' he said. (I'm sure he was calling Chaplin by his christian name by then.)

'You're damn well not,' I said. 'You'll go across to Winchcombe and take your turn like the rest.'

So Hugh went across to Winchcombe and had his other hip done. Two months later, and for the first time in six years, he was walking down the road. It made a tremendous difference to him. He could walk down to the nearest pub, not that he was a great drinker but he did love the company.

He was able to walk far enough with Erica for them to go out to lunch. They could go and sit on the small promenade at Sanford and soak up the sun. They weren't shackled by the house any more. This incredibly courageous couple were able to go on enjoying many happy years together — two living tributes to the miracles of modern medicine.

*   *   *

Mrs Diana Thompson was a smart, Eton-cropped, efficient

career woman, the second senior partner in the largest firm of accountants in Tadchester. She had a Cambridge degree, had come from a wealthy background and was a lady (whatever that means). She certainly had poise and style.

She was severe, unapproachable, abrupt in manner and minded her own business, which was about the biggest sin you could commit in Tadchester. Nobody quite knew what she was up to in her spare time, though a lot made educated guesses. She used to spend her weekends and holidays away from Tadchester. It was rumoured that she had been seen going into a night club in London, but nobody ever really knew.

She had extremely good holidays in expensive places like the West Indies, the Bahamas, Bermuda and the South of France. I knew this, as from time to time I was called on to give her injections and immunisations.

She was certainly not short of money, one of the things she couldn't hide. When her father died, his will was published and he left all his money — a six-figure sum — to her. She must also have had a reasonable salary from her accountancy. She was the first occupier of one of a block of luxury flats built at the western end of Tadchester Quay near the park and art gallery. They were extremely up-market for Tadchester, being walled-off for privacy, and with their own swimming pool. As far as anybody knew she had no male friends.

I was surprised one day to get a call from Mrs Thompson. Would I come and see a guest?

I went at the end of the morning surgery and was shown into the large, double bedroom. As there was a nightdress by the side of the bed and a lady's dressing gown hanging on the back of the door, I assumed she was sharing the bed with the wheezing, overweight male propped up gasping on some lace pillows.

'This is a friend of mine,' she said in her curt tone, giving nothing away and with no feeling of tenderness. 'James Fry. He's come down here so that I can look after him while his chest is bad.'

James Fry turned out to be a fifty-year-old Fleet Street journalist, not a big name but someone who had had to hold his own amongst the big names for a number of years. He had a serious lung complaint which finally reduced him to the extent that he could hardly walk.

There was nobody who looked less like a nurse than Diana Thompson, I doubted if she could be very helpful if he really got ill.

On examining Fry I found that he had a chronic, irreversible lung disease with secondary heart failure. He was on a mass of drugs and had obviously been treated by the best physicians in London. Also, obviously, none of them had been able to do a great deal for him. He had been a heavy smoker as well as having a bad chest, and the combination of the two had almost brought him to a halt.

After examining him I suggested various changes in medication, arranged for him to have some domiciliary oxygen then took Diana into the next room.

'Mr Fry is extremely ill,' I said. 'I think it would be as well to get him under one of the physicians here and see what help we can give you.

'Would you like the District Nurse to call or shall we get in a private nurse?'

'I don't need any help at all,' she said, 'I can manage completely.'

'But you are holding down a job,' I said. 'Can you do both?'

'I can manage that as well,' she said abruptly. She wasn't a person to argue with.

I arranged for my friend John Bowler, a physician at Winch-combe, to come over and see him. His findings were much the same as mine: very little we could do, and no benefit in going to hospital. He thought Fry's outlook was very poor and, when pressed, said he thought he wouldn't last more than about six months.

When Fry had been in Tadchester a few months Diana came to my surgery to say she would like to take him to her cottage in the Dordogne for a month.

'I'm afraid I can't recommend it,' I said. 'He's far too ill to travel. A journey to France could well be too much.'

'He might as well die there as anywhere else,' snapped Diana. 'There's no point in his just stopping at home.'

That was that.

James — as I now knew him — was terribly excited about going. Just the fact that somebody considered that he might make it was a tremendous boost to his morale, and he improved visibly. I kitted them out with enough stuff to see them through any crisis, gave them a letter to give to any doctor if they needed help, and even managed to fix them up with some oxygen cylinders.

They had a month in the sun and he came back better than I could have expected. This only meant that he could walk two or three hundred yards but it was enough to get him to the quay, where he could sit and watch the boats.

They told me there was no need for me to call at the flat any more: if they could get to France they could certainly visit my surgery. So once a month Diana used to drive James over for a check-up.

Over the next six years she called me out only twice to see him. Both occasions were during the winter when he had a chest infection superimposed on his already chronic lung disease.

As James got slowly weaker, Diana organised her office routine so that she was in for only three hours in the morning and two hours in the afternoon.

James's health slowly and steadily got worse. It took only a slight chill or a little over-exertion to make him dangerously short of breath. He was unable to leave the flat at all under his own steam.

He was in a pretty desperate state when they came for medication for their annual holiday to the Dordogne, in his seventh year in Tadchester, but I knew better than to try to persuade them not to go. He came back a little improved, still not well enough to go out and walk on his own, but much better in spirit and with a good tan.

During their next trip to the Dordogne, I wasn't surprised to receive a card from Diana saying that James had died peacefully in the sunshine and was to be buried out there.

She came back completely broken. The normally tight-lipped and composed woman wept on my shoulder.

'Oh, Doctor,' she sobbed. 'Why did he have to go? Why did he have to go?'

'My dear Mrs Thompson,' I said (I had never even reached the stage of calling her Diana), 'by some miracle you were able to give James seven more years of happy life of good quality, more than anybody expected. No nurse, no doctor, no hospital could have given him what you gave.'

'Whatever I gave him,' said Diana, 'is nothing to what he gave me. He was my life, my mainstay. Now there's no point in going on.'

Diana was extremely ill for about four months, acutely depressed and withdrawn. She didn't even go to work; she grieved desperately, was careless over her grooming and she looked lined and older.

I offered to send her to a nerve specialist, but she refused.

She came to see me once every week for some sleeping tablets. I refused to give her the facility of re-ordering herself: I didn't want to tempt her to take too many.

After six months she slowly began to pick herself up again, looking smarter, going back to the office, but she never went out in the evenings or at weekends.

Gradually she inched out of her shell and occasionally she would go up to London. Then one day she called to announce she was finishing with the Tadchester firm of accountants and taking up a post in the metropolis.

'Dr Clifford,' she said, 'I never thanked you for all you did for James and myself. We would never have managed without you.'

I was again able to tell her what a marvellous person I thought she was, that by transfusing someone with her own energy she had given James at least seven extra years of life at no small sacrifice to herself.

'Whatever I gave him,' said Diana, dropping back into her curt manner, 'was nothing to what he gave me. He was my whole life.'

74

How this breathless invalid gave her so much I shall never know. I do know that I saw the near-miracle of a dying man being sustained for seven rewarding years.

CHAPTER 7

Pearls Before Swine

My senior partner Steve Maxwell had instilled in me the importance of routine visits, particularly to the elderly.

'Sometimes the only medicine needed,' he said, 'is for you to sit and listen. You will find in time that it is rewarding to both you and the patient.'

Over the years in Tadchester I built up a number of regular calls, ostensibly to see people who were ill and enquire about their progress. But just as much, it was somewhere I could catch my breath, have a chat, a glass of home-made wine, a cup of tea, swop a few stories, have a good laugh and generally relax.

One such call was at the Coach and Horses, an old thatched coaching inn halfway between Tadchester and Hovery, to see the venerable Mrs Partridge.

In a small fenced garden opposite the inn stood a genuine coach which, some 150 years earlier, used to ply the muddy track which is now tarmacadam road between Tadchester, Winchcombe and Hovery. With its immaculate thatch, black timbers, white walls, polished high-backed wooden seats and solid wood trestle tables, the inn was a favourite holiday spot for the better-breeched holidaymaker. It had a sort of public school

air about it, with the chat in the bar more about Fiona and Hugo and Clarence than Elsie, Gladys and Albert.

I had been in Tadchester for two years when I was summoned to see Mrs Partridge, the lady of the inn. She had got fed up with her elderly doctor, who had a one-man practice out in the country, and wanted somebody younger to look after her.

I had already met her son-in-law, Group Captain Charles Hunter and his vivacious wife Felicity. Charles and Felicity ran the hotel although Mrs Partridge was still a major shareholder. She was an imperious old lady who very much resented the fact that her son-in-law was now running things.

Most of the time, when she was well enough to be up and about, she sat in the corner of the pub slandering her son-in-law, saying that he had stolen all the family money, was running the pub down and she would advise people to go and stay back in Tadchester. The Coach and Horses certainly wasn't what it was in her husband's day.

The truth of the matter was that Charles had not only put his boundless enthusiasm and energy into the hotel and worked it up to its present high standards, but had also invested a great deal of his own money.

The fact that the atmosphere of the pub was public school, and that by some natural selection the guests were usually gin and tonic, hunting, shooting and fishing people, was because the inn really had a public school foundation. The late Mr Partridge had been a housemaster at Repton and when retirement came he fancied running a country hotel.

He brought certain standards to the running of the inn. Guests had to toe the line, much as any boy in his house at school had had to do. You had to dress for dinner and conduct yourself in a gentlemanly manner whatever you were doing, be it drinking, playing darts, or even bowling in the skittle alley.

One day a leather-clad motorcyclist found that you couldn't break the rules. He came into the public bar and asked Mr Partridge, one of the few men who served drinks in the public bar in a morning coat, for a Harvey's Bristol Cream Sherry. Having downed it like an American film star throwing back a snort of whisky, he asked for a second glass. Gulping that down, he asked for a third. He was refused point-blank by the indignant Mr Partridge, who sent him packing — nobody was going to drink sherry like that in his hotel, and to a man who drank liquors before dinner, he muttered audibly 'Pearls before swine.'

Mrs Partridge had a multitude of small things wrong with her, and one or two large things. I developed the habit of going there every Wednesday evening to have a cup of tea — which was served in her bedroom — and a chat. She would be sitting up in her bed waiting for me in a clean white nightgown. I can't ever remember having to examine her other than superficially, and she was perfectly fit enough to be up and about. But when a doctor called you always greeted him in bed ready for an examination, even if you weren't prepared to let him examine you.

We would discuss Mrs Partridge's medical problems, make a few remarks about things like opening bowels and passing water, and then one of the maids would bring in a tray. I would have a cup of tea from a silver teapot, and eat sugar-coated, wafer-thin biscuits. Then she would regale me with tales of the past. Weekend house parties, hunt balls, titled acquaintances, when ladies and gentlemen were ladies and gentlemen.

The second half of my visit would be spent downstairs with Charles and Felicity. In the summer the place was packed with visitors, and there was not time for more than to say hello and have a quick glass of sherry. But in the winter, most often there were just the three of us, and we would sit round a great log fire in the bar and sort out the world's problems.

Under the incongruities of British law, the hotel had to be open the whole year round. Though it was packed in summer, on three nights a week in the winter, the only customer was a patient who was allowed to come out of the local mental hospital on his own, have a pint and then go back again.

Charles had been captain of football and cross-country at Repton. He was a fine figure of a man: 6 foot 2 inches, proportionally well built, jet black hair, and an infectious, raucous laugh. He had been in the RAF during the war, before which he'd spent most of his years in India working for an oil company. He had a great love of flying and his claim to fame was that he was the first man to introduce gliding into India. He paid to have a glider boxed and shipped over, and opened the first Indian gliding club.

His years in the air force had made him unsettled, and after the war he did not want to go back to India. Wandering around England he happened to book in at the Coach and Horses for the night. There he found his old housemaster working behind the bar and the housemaster's daughter, whom he remembered as a gap-toothed little girl, had now blossomed into the beautiful Felicity.

Charles's one-night stay was extended to three weeks. He and Felicity were engaged after a month and married after six.

Pam, myself and the children were among the privileged few who were asked to dine on Boxing Day lunchtime when Felicity would produce such exotic dishes as frogs' legs, snails and caviare.

Charles and Felicity were made joint presidents of the Gaderene Society. This was a society for those of us who were stupid enough to crawl through the surf at night, dragging seine nets, trying to catch fish off the beaches. All members were treated to an annual dinner one night in the winter, when Felicity would produce clams, oysters, exotic fish dishes — everything a self-respecting fisherman would expect to eat — and we would dance, sing and generally let our hair down.

They were kindness itself. One December they asked my help in selecting half a dozen people who would otherwise have had a bad Christmas or no Christmas, to come and spend Christmas Day with them. Not only did they offer to feed these people, but they would also go and pick them up and run them home.

After much searching I could find only four. These included a widowed father and his spastic son; a retired butler, a tall fastidious man who lived in a tiny bedsit; and a decrepit old lady, Mrs Tuckett, who lived in an equally decrepit old cottage just off the Winchcombe road.

The cottage was filthy, and I doubted if she fed herself properly. She would take anything from anybody, and certainly wasn't proud. She was a cheery old soul, though, and made light of the circumstances she was in.

Her nextdoor neighbours did their best for her. They were old themselves, but produced a meal most days. A

Christmas free of the old lady was a blessing on its own.

Mrs Tuckett loved Christmas Day at the Coach and Horses, and went home showered with presents and tins of food. She touched Charles's and Felicity's consciences and they made a habit of popping in with a gift of groceries, usually once a week when they went into Tadchester shopping.

Old Mrs Tuckett was found dead in her cottage one morning, from either a coronary or cerebral thrombosis. I broke the news to Charles and Felicity on my next visit.

They were both very upset. 'Poor old thing,' said Felicity. 'She had so little. There was so much more we could have done for her.'

I smiled. I'd been there when ambulancemen started to look around for blankets and things to lay Mrs Tuckett out. In every conceivable nook and cranny they found pound notes, saving certificates, share certificates and cash bonds. They totalled £37,173.

'Good God!' said Charles, throwing his head back with a great roar. 'She could have bought the hotel.'

One spring, after nine years of my weekly visits, Mrs Partridge died within forty-eight hours of contracting an acute chest infection. She had been a great old character but the way she belittled the efforts of her son-in-law and daughter was very naughty, and I think she knew it. However, I felt a sense of loss. My Wednesday evening call *was* a medical visit. If I wasn't going to see her I was selfishly going out into the country just for a drink. It didn't feel right.

'I do hope you will still come on Wednesdays,' said Felicity.

'I hope so too,' I said. 'But with your mother's going I have no medical excuse.'

'We'll come up next week,' said Felicity. 'Don't stop suddenly — you're part of the scenery.'

I called the next Wednesday. And on the wooden seat by the log fire was a most beautiful leather medical case with the initials R.C. It really was elegant: a case I could never have afforded.

'Just a little memento of mother,' said Felicity. 'Your visits were so important to her. She used to say that it was the high-light of her week.'

I stuttered some modest protest.

'Rubbish,' said Felicity. 'It was so important to her that she started to change her nightdress on a Wednesday after having had Monday as a changing day for eight years. She couldn't pay you a bigger compliment than that.'

I picked up my new case. Would I, I wondered, be changing my pyjamas specially for someone when I was ninety-seven?

* * *

John Denton solved my problems of conscience regarding visits to the Coach and Horses. He suggested that we formed a two-man fishing club, with John as president and me as secretary, and that we should meet fortnightly at the Coach and Horses and apply ourselves to discuss the different aspects of fishing over a drink.

When I first met John Denton he'd given me lessons on coarse fishing, and since then we'd had one or two very enjoyable days on the river. Now I fancied fly fishing for trout.

'But I never seem to find the time, John.'

'Make the time,' he said. 'It's the only way. Otherwise you'll never get round to it. Tell you what, it won't be long before the mayfly hatch.' (It was getting towards the middle of May.) 'I'll give you a couple of lessons and we'll be ready for the river as soon as the hatch starts.'

He gave me a couple of dry-land lessons on a fly rod, using a scrap of cloth on the line instead of a hook. ('I've only got two ears,' he said, 'and I'm rather attached to them. You can have a hook when you've learned to cast without being a danger to the public at large.')

The thickness of the fly line came as a surprise. The nylon monofilament I'd used for tench when John gave me my first fishing lessons, had been almost invisible.

Casting was tricky to start with. There is no weight to rely on as there is in other forms of fishing. The only weight is that of the line itself. To the end of the line John tied a short length of finer line — the *point*, which takes care of any wear and tear — and to this point he tied the cloth.

The rod had a beautiful action, springy right down to the butt without being floppy. And all the work was done from the wrist.

'Take some line off the reel in your left hand,' said John. 'Then take the rod back with your right, over your shoulder to one o'clock. When the line is fully extended behind you, bring the rod smartly forward. Keep doing that, and release a bit more line with every forward cast.'

I felt like a circus ringmaster, waving the rod from the wrist as if I were flicking at a team of performing horses. Indeed, after a few motions there was a crack just like a whip.

'How about that, John?' I asked. 'Hear that crack?'

'I did,' said John. 'Bottom of the class for that. It's what happens if you bring the line forward before it's streamed out fully at the back. Do it too often and you'll finish up without a hook. And though I've not mentioned this before, a hook is by way of being a necessity for catching trout.'

After a while I'd got the hang of it enough to try some target practice, dropping the rod tip when the cloth was about three feet above the desired spot.

One afternoon a couple of days later, John rang me at home.

'I hear you've got the day off, Bob,' he said. 'The mayfly hatch has started. Fancy trying for a couple of trout?'

'Love to. But I'm painting the shed.'

'The shed can wait. The mayfly won't. Make time. Remember? I'll expect you in half an hour.'

I cleaned up quickly, leaving the shed half-painted, and drove over to John's cottage. He was waiting, with rods, landing nets and creels already packed in his Land-Rover.

In a slow eddy of the Tad, the mayfly were hatching. It wasn't so much of a hatch as a transformation.

The mayfly larvae, known to the angler as 'nymphs', rise to the surface after two or three years of living underwater. On the surface their skins split and the adult flies — the 'duns' — emerge. The duns then fly off to bushes on the bank where one more sloughing of the skin leaves them ready to take part in their brief mating dance; after which they return to the water, near to death, as spent flies or 'spinners'.

On the bank, however, there was not much time to worry about the love life of the mayfly. The water was dimpled by ring after ring as trout rose to suck down the emerging flies.

'There y'are, Bob. Not a moment too soon,' said John. 'Dry fly for these. A dry fly floats, just like the hatching mayfly. Drop it upstream and let it float down. When a trout takes, just the merest lift of the wrist will hook it. Don't make a meal out of playing the things; just get 'em back to the bank and have another go.'

He tied a fine point to the end of the line, and to that an artificial fly — red and green, I think it was — made from gamecock hackles. He pressed the fly in a piece of chamois leather which had been lightly soaked in liquid paraffin. ('That's to make sure it floats.') and handed over the rod.

I looked at the fly.

'Doesn't look much like a mayfly to me, John.'

'Doesn't look like one to another mayfly, either. But it does to the trout.'

I made one or two casts, letting the fly float downstream to the end of the swim, without result.

'Don't worry, Bob. Just keep casting,' said John. 'I'm getting out of your way to try my luck further down. Oh, when you catch one, use this.'

He handed me a short, heavy, lead-weighted cosh — a 'priest' — with which to kill the fish painlessly. One swift clout on the back of the head was much more humane than letting them gasp out their lives in the basket.

'Why is it called a priest, John? I keep meaning to ask.'

'It administers the last rites, doesn't it? Joke. Ha, ha. Not one of mine, so don't blame me.'

Several casts later, the water dimpled under the fly and it disappeared. The point of the line disappeared also, knifing swiftly under the surface. I lifted the rod with a quick flex of the wrist — and a trout was on.

There can never be another trout quite like the first one. I

could imagine its muscular body shaking this way and that as it
bore back and forth in its efforts to throw the hook.

Before long I had it close enough to the bank to slip the
landing net under it, and out it came. It turned out later to
weigh about 1¼lb, but to me it was Moby Dick himself.

One clunk of the priest and it was dead, quivering the whole
length of its body. It seemed that almost at once its beautiful

speckled sheen started to fade. I admired it for about half a minute then put it in the creel.

I dried the fly on a piece of amadou (a sort of spongy fungus) which John had left with me and squeezed it between a scrap of oiled chamois.

Ten minutes later, another trout. Fifteen more minutes, a third was bucking and boring on the end of the line. Within an hour and a half I had seven beautiful fish. Then suddenly the rise stopped. That was it for the time being.

'You've done well, young Bob,' said John who returned with five fish. 'This calls for a pint.'

We called at John's local riverside pub, where I immediately began to boast. I spread a piece of cloth on the bar and displayed my seven beauties to the landlord. As he was nodding approvingly, I noticed that two anglers at a corner table were also taking out several trout apiece from their baskets.

'Looks as if someone else has had a good day,' I said.

'Yes,' said the landlord. 'Not a bad start at all to Duffers' Fortnight.'

Duffers' Fortnight? I looked at John, who gulped in his beer.

'Ah, well . . . Yes, Bob lad. It's a name given to the first mayfly rises. Sometimes the trout do get a bit suicidal — er, start rising well. But don't worry, there are Duffers' Fortnights when the fish will look at anything but a mayfly. It's no guarantee. You've done well there, lad. You caught those fish fair and square. If it had been that easy, I'd have come back with more than five now, wouldn't I?'

I felt better for that. I didn't find out until later that he'd spent some of his time checking tickets and chatting to other anglers.

Back home that evening I was greeted like a hero. And I must admit I played up to it, thrilling the family — and finally boring them — with a detailed account of how each fish fought like a fiend until it was finally defeated and brought to the net.

Next day there were trout for tea.

'Congratulations, darling,' said Pam.

'Clever old dad,' said Trevor.

'Cleverest daddy in the whole world,' said Jane.

'Yummm...,' said Paul.

I blushed and ate on. Feeling, for all my undisputed prowess with the rod, a bit of a fraud. Not to say a bit of a duffer...

CHAPTER 8

Ways of Dying

Charlie Sloper, the local poacher, idler and ne'er-do-well, declined quickly after the death of his old friend and adversary Major Hawkins.

For the last few months of the Major's life, Charlie and he were not speaking — the Major had stormed out of the Tadchester Arms after an almighty row — but for Charlie there was always the hope that the Major would return to the pub and that they could resume the trading of insults.

Perhaps the Major had missed Charlie, too. An almost daily argument with the man who had saved his life under shellfire in World War One was not an event to be passed up lightly. But in their last argument Charlie and the Major had mortally insulted each other. And it seemd that 'mortally' was no exaggeration.

Charlie appeared at the Major's funeral, unrecognisable as a spruce, clean, silver-bearded little man in a neatly pressed suit. But within a couple of weeks he was back to his usual garb of tatters and grime.

His behaviour, never the most conformist in the world, grew more and more eccentric. He wandered about Tadchester's new supermarket, openly picking up odds and ends, putting

them in his greasy haversack, and wandering out without attempting to pay. He was never spotted by the manager, who would certainly have had him prosecuted. The check-outs were operated by local girls who knew Charlie, and who let him get away with it either out of compassion or fear. Charlie had taken to sudden rages and, small though he was, made a fearsome spectacle when he erupted.

I had first-hand experience of this when I greeted him one morning in the market square. He was standing by a vegetable stall, possibly waiting for the moment when he could safely purloin a potato or two.

'Good morning, Charlie,' I said.

He turned and glared, crouching like a wrestler with a tightening grip on his knobbly walking stick.

'And 'oo are you?' he hissed.

'Dr Clifford, Charlie. Surely you remember me?'

'Never seen you before in my life!' he yelled, raising the stick. 'Now git orf out of it! Go on. Piss orf!'

I pissed orf.

Charlie's behaviour in the Tadchester Arms worsened as much as it had outside. He would insult everyone who gave him a cheery greeting or a kind word. Often, if a sympathetic regular handed him a bottle of brown ale, his favourite tipple, he would return it to the bar, tell the barman to put the cap back on, and demand to be given the money instead.

He had always been dirty and smelly, qualities which became more evident at close quarters, especially when the pub had warmed up a bit. Now he was getting really beyond endurance. He would sit at a table designed for six people, and all evening there would be five empty seats.

All that was overlooked by the landlord, Geoff Emsworth, whose genial exterior hid a nature as hard as putty. But things came to a head when the public bar was renovated by the brewery. The first stage was the toilets. They were closed down and the public bar customers had to use those in the saloon.

The saloon bar was frequented by some very up-market types indeed, and they did not take at all kindly to having the peasantry stamp through. Least of all did they take kindly to the smelly little apparition wearing one stout brogue and one frayed plimsoll and carrying an old army haversack. But none of them dared say anything to Charlie. From a face as black as a miner's after a hard shift flashed fierce, ice-blue and quite mad eyes. Charlie had become a dangerous man to cross.

In the end, however, Geoff had to call him to order.

'It's bad enough your stinking the place out,' said Geoff, 'and putting paying customers off their ale. I don't even mind you upsetting some of the pucka sahibs in the saloon. Do some of them good to see how the other half lives, if you can call it that. But keep your grubby little mitts off the freebies. Right?'

Geoff's freebies were luxuries not available in the public bar: bowls of peanuts, cheese nibbles and crisps put out on the saloon bar counter to heighten the thirsts of the gentry; and two ornamental bricks, the frogs of which were full of free matches.

Geoff had been unable to understand, especially when the saloon was quiet, how all the bowls and the bricks would suddenly become empty. Then one night he happened to see Charlie returning from the gents.

With a furtive glance to ensure that what few customers there were had their backs to him, Charlie emptied peanuts, cheese nibbles, crisps, matches and all, into his haversack. Then he picked up a half-pint glass from the bar, filled it from the soda syphon, and marched back to his lonely table in the public.

'Just a minute . . .' said Geoff.

'You go makin' accusations like that,' said Charlie, 'and I'll 'ave the Lor on yer. Takin' away my good name.'

'All right, then,' said Geoff. 'Empty your haversack.'

'Piss orf,' said Charlie.

Even that didn't get him banned. Geoff was a patient man. But finally it had to be done, if only for a little while.

The public bar was to be closed for several weeks to allow the renovations to be completed. The regulars then had the choice of drinking in the saloon — a happening much resented by the resident county types — or of finding another pub for the time being.

'Nothing personal, Charlie,' said Geoff. 'But you are definitely not a saloon bar type. I'll have to ask you to stay away, or at least stay in the garden, until the public's done out.'

'That's nice after all the years I've been comin' here,' said Charlie. 'You can stuff your bloody pub. I'll take my custom elsewhere.'

But no other pub would have Charlie's custom. After being thrown out of every one within walking distance — and Charlie was capable of walking quite a way when he put his mind to it — he was back in the garden of the Tadchester Arms. Geoff would serve him through the hatchway, but steadfastly refused to allow him across the threshold.

After a couple of months the public bar was opened again, and Charlie was allowed back in. But it was nothing like the scruffy, cosy, spit-and-sawdust bar he had known. There was a carpet on the floor, soft upholstery on the benches and chairs, a juke box going full blast and a couple of one-armed bandits in constant use.

Worse, the clientele changed. Before long the old regulars deserted the bar and their places were taken by a much younger crowd.

Charlie had nothing in common at all with the youngsters in jeans and mini-skirts, and he winced every time the juke box blared out with another rock 'n' roll record. The youngsters were not nearly so tolerant as the old regulars, and made loud comments about the dirty old geezer in the corner. Visibly Charlie began to age, even to shrink — and he was small enough to begin with.

One night, after closing time, as Geoff went round clearing the tables, he noticed Charlie's haversack slung over the back of a chair.

'Silly old duffer's forgotten it,' Geoff muttered to himself. 'Shall I keep it for him or pretend the bloody thing's been nicked?'

As he reached across to pick it up, he noticed a tattered heap under the table. Charlie.

Though I hate being called out at night for trivial reasons, I am only too glad to turn out for serious cases, and Charlie was serious.

By the time I reached the pub, Geoff had laid him on a bench and loosened his filthy clothes. Charlie's breathing was chillingly shallow and his pulse only a flicker.

'May I use your phone, please, Geoff?' I said. 'We've got to get him to hospital quickly.'

Charlie lived for another month in the hospital. He turned out to be suffering from severe malnutrition and, of all things, dehydration.

Geoff, busy man though he was, visited him every other day with presents of fruit and good wishes from old acquaintances —

though most of the good wishes Geoff used to make up on the spot.

Charlie never thanked him. He recovered enough after ten days to get his old cussedness back and made the lives of the ward staff a misery. He made such a fuss about 'wimmin' gazing upon his scrawny little body that he was bathed only by male nurses.

One night, after a marathon rave at everybody in sight, he simply closed his eyes and died.

The funeral was simple, with only three wreaths. They were inscribed: 'To Charlie, from your friends in the public'; 'From the regulars in the saloon'; and 'From Geoff and Ruby, Tadchester Arms'.

And there was only one mourner: Geoff Emsworth, who had ordered and paid for the three wreaths himself.

'Couldn't have the old lad going as lonely as he'd lived these past few months,' said Geoff. 'Anyway, he should be all right now. He'll have met up with Major Hawkins — if they allow

visitors where Charlie is, and don't mind the stoking being interrupted. Wherever it is, there'll be some right bloody ructions tonight...'

* * *

Nellie Walters, a small but sturdy matron of seventy-eight, came in to see me again about her knee. She suffered from a form of dry eczema, possibly a legacy from her days in service when she spent endless hours on her knees, scrubbing the stone floors of a large house up the hill. The eczema was always there, but now and again would spread in a flaming red and painful patch.

I prescribed the usual cream and then asked, 'And how is your husband?'

'He's going,' said Nellie.

'Going? Going where?'

'Passing away.'

'Oh, dear! I'd better call in and see him this afternoon. But what makes you think he's going?'

'He's had twelve bottles of light ale in the sideboard for three weeks now, and he's not touched a drop.'

This *was* serious. William Walters, pushing eighty-five, had always been fond of his ale. Now and again the walk to the pub became a bit too much for him, so he stocked the sideboard with bottles of light. Never to my knowledge had the bottles survived more than a few days.

Big and portly, but with the ramrod bearing and waxed moustache of one of Kitchener's men, William had seemed indestructible. His clothes, serviced by Nellie, were always clean and brushed. His trouser seams looked as if you could sharpen a pencil on them. And there was always a flower in his buttonhole, backed by a piece of fern with the stem wrapped in damp moss and clipped in a silver holder.

He had run his household like a barrack room. Meals had to be there on time. Not a second early or a second late. None of his five children had ever dared sit down at the table before he did, nor did any of his nine grandchildren when they came to visit. Both children and grandchildren had to stand behind their chairs until William entered the room — scrubbed shiny, moustache waxed and with a fresh flower in the buttonhole — and sat down. Only then were they allowed to sit and bow their heads for grace.

William's indestructibility had defied all the odds. At seventeen he had volunteered for the Boer War, and been turned down for what was described as 'smoker's heart'. Even at that age he smoked full-strength cigarettes, potent enough to make a blast-furnaceman cough. At eighty-four he still smoked them.

In World War One the medical boards were not so fussy, and William was accepted for army service. Because of his age and his five children, he was not among the unfortunate 'volunteers' marched away by the local squire. But in 1916, at the age of thirty-four, he turned up at the Tadchester recruiting office.

'I was no chicken,' he used to tell his drinking pals, 'but they were glad enough to have me.'

From all accounts, William was glad enough to go. It was possibly not so much patriotism as the strain of living in a small house with Nellie and five lively children. Even William's repressive domestic regime couldn't keep the noise down all the time.

Whenever Nellie had presented him with another child, William had gone off to 'wet the baby's head'. The wetting usually took two or three days and he didn't come home until the money ran out, leaving poor Nellie to be looked after by kindly neighbours.

The first child was a boy, and then came three girls. 'This one had better be a boy,' ordered Nellie as she went into labour with the fifth.

Nellie was so scared of his reaction that, when the girl was born, she pleaded with the midwife to tell William it was a boy. The midwife, equally frightened of William, acquiesced. While William was roistering on a head-wetting to end all head-wettings, the poor child was even registered as a boy.

The sobering discovery that it was a girl, the ensuing almighty row, and the trouble involved in getting the child re-registered, may have been what finally sent William off to fight for King and Country.

He joined the Royal Artillery. Such was the need for men on the Western Front that he arrived in France trained in the rudiments of signalling, map reading and gun laying, but not having the first idea of how to use a rifle.

No time was a good time to be in the trenches, but 1916 was a worse year than most. Soon, Gunner Walters was being carried to a field hospital. Even in the filth of the trenches — and even without Nellie in attendance — William was still a dandy. The medical orderlies were amazed at the cleanliness of his body and underclothes. The body, though clean and free from lice, had

been bashed about enough to qualify for a Blighty One. And William was shipped across to a military hospital near Dover.

Back in France a few months later, he was blown up again. This time he was carried into the field hospital wearing the remains of a monk's robe over his khaki.

'I'd got tired of being shot at,' he told me. 'And I came across this dead monk. What he was doing there I'll never know, but he certainly didn't need his robe any more. So I borrowed it. It was lovely and warm, but I was really hoping that the Germans would have some respect for the cloth.'

William had taken the additional precaution of sleeping in an old water tower, the only structure left standing for miles, on the premise that if the Boche hadn't hit it so far, they weren't likely to now.

He was wrong. A shell landed in the tower and blew him right out of it. Neither he nor anybody else knew how he survived the blast and the 30-foot parabola to the ground. His injuries even after that weren't too serious, but again enough to qualify for a Blighty One.

William had never been much of a hand at writing and Nellie hadn't heard from him for weeks. Then one day she met one of his pals, also in the Artillery, home on leave.

'Have you seen anything of my William?' she asked. (Nobody ever called him Bill, incidentally. Nobody who valued his front teeth, that is.) 'I'm worried sick about him.'

'He's all right, Nellie,' said the gunner. 'You should know anyway — you've had him home twice on sick leave.'

'The swine,' said Nellie through clenched teeth. 'If he's been home, he's never got as far as here.'

Nor had he. William's amazing powers of recovery, reinforced by the sight of the lovely young nurses, soon had him out of bed. He was back in bed as soon as he found a nurse compliant enough to join him, and he spent the rest of both leaves wenching and drinking.

His third wound was a terrible one. But again, comparatively speaking, he was lucky.

Sitting in a trench with six of his mates, he bent down to open a tin of beans. As he did so, a shell or mortar bomb landed. The fragments went across his back like a monstrous cheese grater, taking off most of the skin and some of the flesh.

A stretcher party found him bent double, unconscious, bleeding horribly and with a tin of beans and a tin opener still clutched in his hands. All that was left of his six mates were the legs and lower trunks, still sitting on empty ammunition boxes.

I don't know in detail what techniques of patching up or plastic surgery were used in the First World War. Certainly they worked on William, but the results were not very pretty. Fifty years on, his back was sound enough, but it looked like a badly made patchwork quilt, with strips of brown, yellow and dead-white skin jumbled together in a haphazard and rough-ploughed pattern.

It was the end of the war for William and this time he did

come home, to be tended with unstinting devotion by Nellie until he was well enough to get up to his old tricks again.

(It says a lot for heredity that Harry Walters, William's grandson, had the same penchant for wenching and boozing, and finished up in my hands several times needing treatment for the result of his escapades.)

When I called on the afternoon of Nellie's visit to the surgery, William was past any form of roistering. I was shocked by the change as I examined him. He was pale, crumpled and shrunken. Even his moustache, left unwaxed for the first time in fifty years, drooped forlornly.

'Help yourself to a drink, Doctor,' he said, gesturing feebly towards the sideboard. 'Plenty there, I've lost the taste for it.'

I knew what Nellie meant. William would not be with us long.

Nor was he. A fortnight later, after a massive but mercifully brief heart attack, he was gone.

A couple of days after the funeral, Nellie got around to sorting out their affairs. Her middle-aged son, a stable and prosperous Tadchester greengrocer, came over to help. And it was as well that he did.

In William's trunk of souvenirs, Nellie came across faded sepia photographs of several ladies she did not recognise, each photograph inscribed with sentiments far from platonic.

'Look at these!' she exploded, waving the photographs in a trembling fist. 'What *did* that man get up to?'

'Give them to me, mother,' said her son, thinking quickly. 'They're nothing at all. All the troops used to be given photographs of girls who came over on concert parties. The frontline troops never even met the girls; the photos used to come up with the rations. Now go and make yourself a cup of tea and I'll see to the rest.'

In the trunk were bundles of letters, more photographs and a couple of inscribed cigarette cases which indicated that William's war service had not been all mud, blood and bullets. Nor had his ravaged back been any obstacle in time of peace.

There was enough evidence to have had him divorced a dozen times over, were he still around.

The son heavily censored the trunk's contents and took the offending items home for burning.

He told me later that as he threw the letters one by one on the garden incinerator, he had been filled with a grudging admiration for his father's exploits.

'The old bugger,' he said. 'All those years he'd been drilling into us kids the virtues of discipline, fidelity and moderation in all things. And look what he'd been up to...'

There was another shock for Nellie when she went to the bank to check on the joint account she kept with her husband. Every week for years she had saved from their pensions and put the money in the bank. She never saw the statements.

'Leave them to me,' William had said. 'Women don't understand things like that.'

At the bank, the clerk pored over the ledger sheets.

'Your account, Mrs Walters? Let's see now ... ah, yes: a balance of seventeen pounds, three shillings and sixpence.'

'Seventeen pounds, three shillings and sixpence!' Nellie exploded. 'But I've been putting money in every week for years, every pension day!'

'Ah, yes, Mrs Walters. But remember that your husband used to come in every week and draw money out. It did seem a strange arrangement, but apparently you were happy to have it that way.'

Nellie stood there rigid, quivering and speechless. William had done it again.

'We haven't seen your husband for two or three months,' said the clerk. 'Is he all right?'

'All right?' repeated Nellie, dazedly.

'Yes...er... I mean, where is he now?'

'Where is he now?' said Nellie, lapsing for a moment from her normal temperate language. 'The swine is where I can't bloody get at him!'

Several years later I was chatting to Nellie, herself then towards the end of her life, about William.

'He gave me some problems, that one,' she said. 'But I knew I had married a man, not an angel with a carnation in his buttonhole. And at least I have one consolation: in all that time he was never unfaithful to me.'

'Yes,' I said, trying not to look shifty. 'You certainly had that to be thankful for.'

*　　*　　*　　•

Two of my favourite patients were Mick and Alice. They'd been married more than fifty years and put the secret of their success down to 'a bloody good row' at least twice a week.

Twelve months earlier, Alice had almost died from a bad bout of pneumonia. They were an independent old pair, and Alice had always made little of her ailments. What had started as a mild 'flu was left to 'work itself out'. By the time I was called in it had worked itself up into something much worse.

Alice's recovery — and Mick's survival, because he was not the most domesticated of men — was due as much to the care of their married daughter Phil (short for Philomena) as to any of my ministrations. After a couple of tense weeks, with poor old Mick a frightened and bewildered spectator, Alice pulled round.

The event was signalled by a bloody good row one morning when Mick forgot to make Alice's breakfast. After sitting on the edge of the bed in anticipation for forty minutes, Alice went down to see how Mick was faring. He was faring very well, sitting with his nose stuck in the sports section of the morning newspaper, drinking tea from a pint mug, with poor Alice's breakfast completely forgotten.

'Even as our rows go, that was a good 'un, Doctor,' said Mick. 'I knew straightaway she was back on form.'

Now, a year later, it was Mick I was worried about. Phil was visiting them one day when she heard strange noises coming from the upstairs toilet.

'What's the matter with dad?' she asked Alice.

'He's been having a lot of trouble on the toilet lately,' said Alice, 'Reckons it's piles. I don't know, though...'

Phil listened from the bottom of the stairs to stifled cries of real pain and muttered gasps of, 'Oh, no...! Jesus, Mary and Joseph...!'

'That's not piles,' she said. 'Have him ready in the morning. I'm taking him to the doctor's.'

Protesting his fitness, Mick was ushered into the surgery by Phil.

'You're poorly, dad,' said Phil. 'Now be told. I've not brought you all this way for nothing. Tell the doctor about your pains.'

'I don't like to,' said Mick. 'Not in front of you. It's private.'

'That's all right, Phil,' I said. 'Just leave us two chaps alone and we'll soon get to the bottom of it.'

Ten minutes later I wished I'd chosen a more fortunate phrase. Even as a sick joke, that was not funny.

Mick had been having pain and increasing difficulties going to the toilet. I followed my brief internal examination by making an urgent appointment for Mick to see Henry, my surgical partner.

Henry confirmed my fears, Mick had a growth of the lower bowel, a condition which, if caught reasonably early, has a good outlook, and the meticulous Henry would have almost guaranteed a cure. We would now have to wait until the operation to assess Mick's chances.

Major operations at Tadchester Hospital were a team effort. Henry operated assisted by Ron Dickinson, with me helping Jack Hart with the anaesthetic and being responsible for saline and blood transfusions that were part of many major operations, as well as making myself generally useful.

Mick's operation lasted five hours; he had come too late, the growth had spread and all Henry could do was to lessen any chance of obstruction, and remove as much of the growth as possible.

'I'm afraid Mick's time is running out,' said Henry, as he wearily put in the final closing stitches.

'How long do you give him?' I asked.

'He will do well if he lasts twelve months,' said Henry.

102

Mick survived the operation but was left extremely weak and debilitated.

I had to break the news to Phil and left it to her own good sense whether or not to tell her mother.

Rightly so, she did; the family had been through some hard times together in earlier years and was well used to accepting harsh facts and coping with them.

A bed was made for Mick in the living room and a cheery fire was kept burning. He was kept well supplied with his favourite reading — pulp Westerns — and in the evenings he would sit in his own armchair and watch television.

He and Alice were both staunch Roman Catholics, well-loved members of St Malachy's Church, and their religion was a great comfort. Father Daly, the parish priest, would call round to discuss with Mick the latest football results and the prospects of horses in the forthcoming races. He would call again once a week to give Mick Communion and hear his confession, not that the poor old lad had much to confess.

I am by no means a religious man, let alone a Catholic, but perhaps faith like Mick's is contagious. During his agonies, I found myself in Liverpool at a conference, and visited the Roman Catholic cathedral. Inside, bathed in a cool, dim, almost underwater light which came in through the windows, it had a peace and calm authority I have seldom come across anywhere else. Sceptic that I am, I found myself kneeling in a pew and saying a short prayer for Mick: 'Please, God, if at all possible, a miracle. If not, no pain.'

As an added bonus to Mick's home comforts he had his 'girlfriends': three local nuns who used to turn up with fruit, cowboy books, and often a bottle or two of Guinness. Such was the eagerness with which Mick looked forward to his girlfriends' visits, and such was the laughter coming from the living room at times, that Alice, bless her, actually got jealous.

'Well,' she said, 'he wasn't always old and poorly, you know. He was a bit of a devil as a lad, that one.'

The bloody good rows went on. I called round one evening to find the living-room window panes vibrating with the ding-dong going on inside. Mick had wanted to catch the sports results on the television and Alice was insisting on watching a soap opera. That was all, but it sounded like a full-scale riot.

'Don't you worry, Doctor,' said Phil, who was making a cup of tea in the kitchen, not bothered in the least. 'My mother knows what she's doing. A row bucks my dad up no end. He's not a little invalid any more, lying there feeling sorry for himself. He's master in his own house, laying down the law.'

Full marks to Alice for applied psychology. And it certainly worked. Six months passed, twelve months. Mick was still with us, enjoying visits from Phil, her husband Jim and their two young children; Father Daly; the nuns; friends, neighbours and relatives — and having a row with Alice whenever things got too quiet.

Mick had no illusions. Early on in the illness, after a sudden twinge of pain, he said to Alice, 'I'm dying, love, aren't I?'

'Don't be so daft,' said Alice brusquely, turning her face away. 'I've got a nice bit of mince for your tea, and you're not missing that.'

'It's all right, love,' he said. 'You don't have to kid me. I'm on the transfer list all right. But I'm not complaining; I've had a good run.'

After about fifteen months came the inevitable decline. Even with pain relievers and heavy sedation Mick was in great discomfort and would have restless nights which he sweated through determined not to wake Alice upstairs. Alice herself was not too well. Her devotion to Mick was unstinting and she was becoming worn out.

'It might be best,' I said to Phil, 'if we thought about moving your father to hospital now. He'll get every attention there, and it will take this enormous strain off your mother.'

'He wouldn't take too kindly to that,' said Phil. 'He hates hospitals. But I tell you what he might accept — a bed at St Bernadette's Hospice.'

In Tadchester was a Roman Catholic Hospice for the terminally ill. It was run entirely on money accrued from massive fund-raising activities and publicity stunts which didn't even stop short at nuns entering sponsored roller skating marathons. Though equipped with hospital facilities, it was not a hospital. Its function was to care for people who were past hope of recovery — not only Catholics, either — and to make their last days tranquil, even happy.

There was no strict routine. Mobile patients could come and go as they pleased during the day, and guests — which is how the patients were regarded and treated — were free to wander from room to room on social visits.

There was an atmosphere of calm and serenity about the place and oddly (or perhaps not oddly at all) a cheerfulness as well; an atmosphere personified by the smiling nuns who moved quietly about their business of tending the terminally ill.

Mick needed a couple of days to think about the Hospice. Though he knew he could not live long, he still had to make a big mental adjustment to move into a place specifically devoted to the actual act of dying.

Finally he agreed. 'With all those nuns I'll be better off for girlfriends than ever,' he said.

'I'm keeping my eye on you, lad,' said Alice.

Phil and Alice went to see him every day at the Hospice, and he still had all his other regular visitors. The nuns really were saintly characters and did a great deal to help Mick prepare himself for the inevitable.

For a couple of weeks the bloody good rows went on, causing the nuns to glide silently away whenever they heard the first warning shots. This was effective family therapy, and they recognised it as such. But as Mick's pain increased, so did the doses of morphine, and he would sit up in bed perfectly relaxed and happy, smiling so contentedly that Alice knew he didn't need the rows any more.

One evening he died. Quietly, and smiling. The morphine had taken care of his pain. Father Daly and the nuns had taken care of his fears. Jesus, Mary and Joseph had given him comfort and strength all his life, and now in death he had gone serenely to meet them.

* * *

Alice, though heartbroken by Mick's departure, took comfort from his way of going, and held up well for the funeral. Even then, her old sense of humour did not desert her.

She was helped into the church by the undertaker, a family friend for whom Mick had once worked. She was weak and frail, and her steps were faltering, but the undertaker held her firmly so that she would come to no harm.

'Don't go spreading rumours about us two,' she said in an aside to Phil. 'He only wants me for my body.'

CHAPTER 9

A Fate Worse than Death

As Medical Officer to Drake's College in Tadchester, a boys' boarding school that had been built up from fifteen to three hundred boys in eleven years by my friend George Tonbridge, I had a range of problems that I didn't meet generally in the rest of the practice. Many of the boys came from abroad and, particularly at the beginning of each year, there was that complicated and heart-rending condition to deal with: home-sickness.

Every October term I had to wade through seventy or eighty routine medical examinations on the new boys. Though most tedious, it was worthwile. There were always half a dozen boys with either one or no testicles, hernias, perhaps a blind eye that had been missed in the past, and the occasional one with some heart condition. Nearly all those with something wrong turned out to be sons of doctors. As with my own children, being the child of a doctor can have many disadvantages: you either over-whelm them with treatment or miss them out altogether.

Drake's College, for all its newness, with an enthusiastic staff and high *esprit de corps*, was soon competing at all levels with much bigger schools at rugby, cricket, swimming and athletics. For one period the First XV went for seventeen matches

without defeat. Good schoolboy rugby is probably the best of all to watch and I used to go and cheer them from the touchline whenever my duties as President of the Tadchester Rugby Club permitted me to.

The First XV had become a tough, sophisticated, organised unit and their seventeenth victory was over a very vigorous Old Boys XV. The Old Boys had a ground in London and the Drake's team were allowed to play them as the last fixture on a short tour of London-based schools. They were entertained after the match and the enlightened headmaster, George, had allowed them to spend a night on the town with the Old Boys — to acquire, he said, a bit of worldly knowledge.

After that night, their rugby skills went to pot. From being a brilliant, well-oiled machine, they had become tired and dispirited. They lost three games in a row, two of them to sides that the Second XV would normally have beaten. Haggard and jaded they had lost spirit not only in their rugby but also in their schoolwork and general life as well. They were fifteen very worried boys.

After a chat with the distraught games master, I asked the team captain to come and see me. He was so adamant that there was nothing wrong that I knew there must be, but there was little I could do except watch and wait.

The following week I got my answer. The scrum-half, a short, ginger-haired boy from Wales, asked Matron if he could see me, privately and confidentially, after the next surgery.

He was reluctant to talk when he first came in, hanging his head. I made some preliminary small talk about the fortunes of the First XV and then asked how could I help him.

He stood there looking tense and desperate, and then burst into tears. Something was very seriously wrong.

'Come on, lad,' I said. 'What is it?'

'I'm giving all the others away, Doctor, but I must tell you. I'm afraid we've all got venereal disease.'

Although this was not impossible, it was very unlikely.

'And where do you think you got it from?' I said.

'We got it in London...from prostitutes,' he said.

Oh dear. Perhaps he was right after all.

'And how does it affect you? Does it hurt when you pass water?'

'Nothing like that,' he said, 'but it's awful — I'm almost too ashamed to show you.'

'Come on,' I said, 'down with your pants. Let's see what the trouble is.'

Shamefully, half-covering his most private parts with his

hand, he lowered his pants. There, in each groin, spreading down into the thigh and on the inner half of his scrotum were large areas of red, sticky skin.

'It's terrible. Will I go blind, Doctor? What shall I tell my parents?' he stuttered between strangled sobs.

'Put your trousers back on,' I said, 'and tell me how you contracted this.'

'Well,' he said, 'the Old Boys took us to a night club . . . and then there was a stripper . . . and then . . . [amongst more sobs] she came and sat on three or four of us — on our knees. A few days later nearly all the team came out in this — we must be giving it to one another.'

'You bunch of lunatics!' I said, struggling not to laugh. 'What you've got is a very common condition called Dhobi's Itch. It's nothing to do with venereal disease. It's a fungal infection in the groin that athletes get through sweating and showering. I've seen fifty boys with it already this term — and none of them had been near a stripper. You've all worried for nothing. For God's sake, why didn't you see me earlier? Some powder and ointment will clear that up and you'll be as good as new.'

He looked at me as if he'd won the football pools.

Word spread like fire. As I was just about to go, the other fourteen players arrived at the surgery.

'Sorry we're late, Doctor. Could we just see you for a minute?'

Each produced identical red areas in the groin. Their relief that they'd only got a small fungal condition in their groins was indescribable, after spending sleepless nights worrying about VD. They were back on form the following Saturday and thrashed their local rivals 37–3.

* * *

Not sleeping, or sleeping too much were among the commonest conditions I met in general practice. A great number of people came for various forms of sleeping tablets. The commonest cause of not sleeping was having formed a habit of waking up

110

too early and I was a believer in giving short, sharp courses of tablets to ensure a full night's slumber.

I probably had no more than my fair share of insomniacs, but I seemed to have more than my share of people who couldn't stay awake. Nearly every day somebody would come in convinced that there was something medically wrong with them because they felt so sleepy and tired all the time. Many of them claimed to have sleeping sickness. I had to explain that you had to be bitten by a tse-tse fly before you could acquire this condition and, as far as it was known, there weren't too many tse-tse flies in Somerset. The likely commonest cause was boredom or anxiety. In the whole of my medical life I've only met one man where sleepiness or too much sleeping was the actual condition. The disturbances in the sleep pattern were usually not an illness in themselves, but were symptoms of some other thing that was going wrong: very often financial trouble, trouble at work or at home.

The heaviest sleeper of them all was Frank Preston, a charge-hand at the electronics factory. He prided himself that he'd been never late for work since the factory opened, there every day at 7.15 sharp. But he did complain that he seemed to fall asleep at every opportunity and that once he was asleep it was very difficult to rouse him.

I did what I could for Frank, but I was much more concerned for his wife, Jenny, who insisted that she was going to have her second baby at home in spite of the fact that she had had a difficult forceps delivery with her first baby in hospital. I tried to persuade her to go to Winchcombe to have the baby but she insisted that she was going to have it at home.

'If you don't want to come, don't, Doctor,' she said. 'I'll manage on my own.'

Even the indomitable Nurse Plank, a stalwart support at home confinements, was worried about it.

However, the ante-natal time went perfectly well, with no complications. The baby was in a good position, and on time Jenny went into labour.

I was called at about 11 o'clock at night to say she was getting on well, but that I had better come along in case a hand was needed. She wasn't quite fully dilated and ready to push when I got there. Jenny was in a large high-ceilinged room with two single beds in it. Her bed was in the middle of the room, its head against one wall, and the other bed with a heap of bedclothes on it stood against one of the side walls.

Jenny did extremely well until the last stage and then she shouted the rooftops off.

The baby wouldn't come the last inch or so and I had to call in Jack Hart to give Jenny a whiff of chloroform while I put some low forceps on and lifted the baby's head out.

Jenny had a fine baby girl. After a couple of stitches, she was as fit as a flea, sitting up in bed and cuddling her newborn. Her mother-in-law came up from downstairs with a cup of tea, and Mrs Preston, Nurse Plank, myself and Jenny sat round chatting. We'd worked hard. We'd been there nearly all night and it was just approaching 6.30 in the morning. Suddenly an alarm clock went off with a shrill clatter next to the bed covered with a heap of bedding. A hand snaked out of the bedding and turned the alarm off.

'Good God!' I said, startled out of my wits. 'What's that?'

'Don't worry,' said Jenny. 'It's only Frank.'

A tousled head appeared above a mound of bedclothes, looking in complete disbelief at the group of people thronging his bedroom. 'Frank,' said Jenny, 'you've got a lovely little girl.'

'Thank God for that,' said Frank. 'When I first saw all these people I thought I had woken up on Tadchester Station.'

*　　*　　*

It was too late to go to bed when I got home so I took Pam up a cup of tea, got myself a bacon sandwich and arrived at the surgery a bit early.

'Oh, I'm glad you're early, Doctor Bob,' said Gladys, 'We've got a man who hasn't an appointment but insists on being seen. Would you mind fitting him in before the surgery?' 'Fine,' I said. 'Give me five minutes then send him in.'

My first patient was a cocky, independent little man who did

the garden at the local convent. 'Won't keep you a minute, Doc,' he said. 'I'd just like something for my knee.'

'What's the matter with your knee?' I asked. 'I don't think I've seen it.'

'No, no, you haven't,' he said. 'But I've got a touch of anthracite.'

This I had to see.

'Hop on the couch,' I said, 'and let's have a look.'

He had a large swollen knee.

'How long,' I asked, 'do you think you've had anthracite of the knee?'

'Oh, about two or three weeks,' he said. 'My mother's got it — or my mother used to have it.'

'Well,' I said, 'I hate to disappoint you, but what you've got is a bit of *arthritis* of the knee. The only time you can get anthracite of the knee is if you sit too close to the back-boiler in your kitchen.'

The sarcasm was lost on him. He accepted my tablets with some disdain and went off happy, convinced that he was being treated for that very common condition — anthracite of the knee.

* * *

113

Aubrey Cattermole looked normal enough when he came into the surgery. Smartly dressed, he carried a trendy executive briefcase in his left hand and had a well-cut trench coat over his arm. His right hand was bandaged.

'Take a seat, won't you?' I said.

'Thank you, Doctor,' he said, glancing vaguely this way and that, although the chair was directly in front of him.

'Ah,' he said, finally locating it. He stepped towards it, caught his coat on the back and knocked it over.

'Oh dear. Silly me,' he said. He then attempted to pick up the chair with his bandaged hand, winced, and tried with the other hand which was still holding the briefcase. Briefcase, coat and chair got into a terrible tangle, resulting in the kind of pantomime act which usually involves a drunk and a deckchair.

'Allow me,' I said, walking round the desk, separating him and his encumbrances from the chair, and setting it back on its feet.

'Most kind,' said Aubrey, sitting in the chair, placing his briefcase on the floor and draping his coat over the top of it. The briefcase toppled over and there was another pantomime session as he tried to right it and replace the coat one-handedly.

'What seems to be the trouble? The hand, I take it?'

'Yes, Doctor. I lit a cigarette at work this afternoon and stupidly flicked the match into the wastepaper basket. I hadn't noticed it was still alight. The basket went up in flames and I tried to beat them out with my hand. Burned it rather badly. It was treated in the first-aid room, but I think it might need looking at properly.'

The hand was blistered pretty badly. I cleaned it, covered it with burn gell and re-dressed it.

'Quite a bruise on your temple there, too,' I said. 'Did you do that trying to put the flames out?'

'Er... no, Doctor. I bumped into a door jamb at home this morning. Nothing serious.'

'Here, I'll prescribe some cream for that to get the swelling down. Anything else?'

'No. My big toe was painful for a while, but it seems to have settled down now.'

'Toe?'

'Yes. I stubbed it on the bed leg a few days ago.'

'I'd better have a look while you're here.'

The toe was badly discoloured, but there was no swelling, and a little manipulation established that nothing was broken or dislocated.

'You seem to have been in the wars lately,' I said.

'Yes... the landlord in my local was saying that only the other night after the pile of pennies on the bar fell on me. Pure

115

accident, of course. I must have caught them with my elbow as I turned round.'

'You'd had a few, had you?'

'No. I'd only just gone in. The wife had sent me to the pub to get me out of the house. She was a bit peeved because I'd broken her favourite vase.'

I was looking at a walking, talking natural disaster area.

'I'd take it steady from now on,' I said. 'And be careful crossing the road.'

'I certainly will, Doctor. I always look both ways. Ha, ha. Well, thanks a lot.'

He stood up, knocking the chair over backwards as he did so, and then repeated the earlier performance as he rescued coat and briefcase.

'Thanks again, Doctor. Bye . . .'

He tucked the briefcase under his right arm, grasped the door handle with his left, and jerked the door open. Straight back into his face.

That abnormal was normal I'd accepted. But Aubrey was more normally abnormal than anyone I'd seen that day.

'Just a minute, Mr Cattermole,' I said. 'Could you spare me another five minutes?'

I asked a few questions about his seeming accident proneness. Casting his mind back, he reeled off incident after incident in which he'd knocked things over, tripped over things, set fire to things, cut himself, bruised himself, winded himself and almost killed himself. It was a habit of his wife to send him out to the pub just to get him out of the house and prevent his doing any more harm to the furniture, fixtures and fittings.

It sounded very much like a particular disease of the nervous system, a condition which manifests itself by lack of co-ordination, clumsiness and a general pre-disposition to accidents.

I booked him in at the hospital for some aptitude and co-ordination tests which later confirmed my diagnosis. He was treated with a drug which corrected his nervous circuitry, and he recovered from his tendency to go bumping around.

But at the moment I was faced with this apparently upright and responsible citizen who couldn't even get out of a room without doing himself some damage.

'When these tests are done,' I said, 'I'm sure we'll be able to give you something to cut down the number of accidents. I hope they don't affect you too much at work.'

'As a matter of fact, they do,' he said. 'I get a bit tired sometimes of people laughing behind my back. And often in front of my face. A bit embarrassing in my position.'

'What position's that, then?'

'I work in the public relations department at Tadchester Electronics,' he said. 'But I'm also unpaid Safety Officer...'

CHAPTER 10

Trouble at Mill

There were problems in Tadchester.

After the coal mine had shut, a government inducement had attracted an electronics firm to work there. This had absorbed some of the redundant work force and had offered many new jobs for women. Then, just as the ex-miners started to drift away, one of the big international chemical companies decided that there was still some life in the slagheaps that surrounded the village of Thudrock, and Thudrock colliery, and a huge works was built to convert the slagheaps into plastic.

Over a period of two or three years after the mine closed down, the two new places of employment actually brought labour into the area. The town boomed and the population slightly increased. As the electronics company was part of a larger corporation it brought in a proportion of skilled men and middle management people to run it.

But then there was unrest over pay at the plastic works and, owing to some worldwide recession, there was a reduction in demand for electronic components. This resulted in a reduction in staff and some redundancies at the electronics works.

Both these two aspects of industrial unrest brought new medical problems.

The trouble at the plastics factory was over pay. I never knew the details. Both the employers and the work force claimed to have right on their side. There were go-slows and processions in the town, and the pubs were full of excited men intent on showing their virility and industrial muscle. If their demands were not met on the following Monday, they said, they would be out on strike. They would show the bosses. Somehow it seemed to give a new awareness to the town. The atmosphere was buoyant.

The demands weren't met and the strike began, with picketing and a general air of euphoria.

Only one or two older people remembered earlier strikes, particularly the miners' strike of 1926.

One old collier told me in the surgery, 'Nobody wins in a strike, Doctor, whether it's right or wrong. You lose money while you are out, the wife and the kids suffer, and when you get back you very rarely make it up.'

Perhaps somebody, someday, will devise some other means of settling industrial disputes which will do less damage to both sides.

The strike had full union backing and at first everybody was full of beans. The strikers' cause and enthusiasm seemed unbeatable.

But this enthusiasm lasted barely two weeks. If you asked any of the strikers how things were going, they seemed as determined as ever. But they weren't as cheery; the excitement had gone. The first week there had been income tax repayments but these were smaller the second week, and with so many commitments like hire purchase on televisions, washing machines and cars people began to wonder how long they could go on. The cheerful, virile strikers now were subdued; the pubs had started to empty. I had more and more worrying mums coming into the surgery about one thing or another, but their basic reason was the lack of security and increasing shortage of money.

After the strike had been on for four weeks there was almost complete demoralisation. Although the strikers were still vehement about their cause and the pickets were still at the factory gate, it was as if the work force had been humiliated. Moneywise, many were in dire straits, and it would be a very, very long time before they recovered from the financial setback, whatever the pay rises.

The strike was finally settled after six weeks. The workers gained practically all they had taken action for and it was almost certainly justified.

What effect it had on the company I have no idea. They were part of a huge international concern, but it certainly cannot have helped them.

The strike left its aftermath. This was the first really serious industrial upset in Tadchester for many a year. Apart from the economic problems it gave people, it left a wake of uncertainty that took a couple of years to finally subside.

People were depressed. Their basic security had been challenged and it showed in many different forms. And the pattern of life had been disturbed.

Men being at home for six weeks with nothing to do, proved to be a strain in some households. A number of marriages broke up, not because of the financial difficulties, or because the partners agreed or disagreed about the strike, but because there was a new aspect to their married life: the husband, the breadwinner, was humiliated by being at home. He had been under his wife's feet for six weeks and their relationship had changed.

I hadn't realised that one little strike in such a small place could have such deep and long-lasting effects. And I remembered the words of my old collier: 'Nobody wins'.

*   *   *

The redundancies at the electronics plant were mainly among the unskilled labourers. To some it was a bonus. They were given redundancy pay and there were plenty of seasonal and other jobs to be found.

The nature of their work, whoever they worked for, hardly changed, so working in one place differed little from many others and a change of scene suited many of them very well.

The worst casualties were among the middle management, the men aged between forty-five and fifty-five; those who had travelled down from large cities, perhaps from London, when the electronics works was first opened.

They had uprooted themselves and come to work in Tadchester. It meant new homes, and new schools for their children. They had settled themselves into the community, perhaps joined the golf club. They became accustomed to eating out, company cars, and a good standard of living. There were perhaps not more than a dozen involved, but at least six of them ended up at my surgery. Here again I had new medical conditions to deal with.

As with the strikers, these men were humiliated — not only because they were no longer wanted in their jobs, but also because they didn't know what to do with their lives from then on. These men of substance and standing were suddenly taken out of the day-to-day battle of earning a living. They retired on reasonable pensions, but there were no more perks and they had nothing to do.

They were also virtually unemployable. Their special skills lay in one particular type of electronics, and I had men in their prime condemned to a life of golf, gardening, and pottering about their homes. A move away would be difficult. The house prices in Tadchester were less than they were elsewhere, and to venture forth into a new area was therefore virtually impossible.

Two of my six managed fairly well. They had an interest in music which they were able to expand. There were several light orchestras in the area which played at local operettas and various concerts, some of which brought in a modest financial return.

I did my best for the other four men, all leading figures who had cut a dash in the community but who were now humbled and had nothing to look forward to. There was little that I could offer, other than tranquillisers, night sedation, and suggestions of pursuing hobbies and taking up other interests.

They were crippled as surely as a man who has had both legs amputated.

I discovered that industrial unrest presented medical problems of its own, and I found I was almost groping in the dark trying to find solutions.

I depended heavily on my senior partner, Steve Maxwell, for advice and guidance. He was probably the wisest, kindest man I have ever known and rather than just catch him for a few minutes at coffee, I asked him if he could come and dine one evening and spare an hour or two in unravelling problems.

Having Steve to dinner was always a great pleasure. He was good company, laughed uproariously at my jokes, was appreciative of Pam's cooking and very good with the children.

Pam left us with our coffee after dinner and got on with the washing up.

'Well, Bob,' said Steve. 'What are these great problems you have? How can we put the world to rights for you?'

'It's mainly things I don't understand,' I said. 'I don't understand why with a fixed population that we see more and more patients.

'With the strikes and redundancies we seem to be having new diseases which I feel at a loss to cope with. I remember some years ago you telling me the answer to society's problems was better individuals but we don't seem to have made much progress.'

'I think there are two major factors,' said Steve. 'First, over the past four or five decades society has changed more than it did over the previous five or six hundred years. Up to and after the First World War the vast majority of people worked for somebody. We were all sheltered, or most of us, by umbrellas. For generation after generation families would work in the same environment. Society was very much in groups and there was somebody at the head of each group or community who would take the responsibility for us.

'Now there is just about only the doctor and the Citizens' Advice Bureaux who are directly available for advice and counselling.

'Although we have a comprehensive social service system with psychologists, social workers and psychiatric workers, experience can't be learned from books. A young man in his twenties with a degree in psychology or sociology, however intelligent he might be and however able, can only have had a certain amount of experience of life and life situations.

'We're at a time of evolution where individuals are becoming freer to express their own ideas. They're not quite sure yet how to do it or whether or not they should do it or even if they want to do it — at least a good number of them.

'The other point is that we are going through a new industrial revolution. Technology is changing and it looks as if, progressively, in the future, machines will do the work and men will be less necessary. We are already at a stage where machines make machines. We have yet to accept that there is a new industrial revolution and tackle the problem in a new way. I don't think anyone's going to go around breaking up looms this time.

'We can't necessarily call it progress: man will always keep moving on to new projects and new ideas. What we have to decide is how to utilise this time we have. To be unemployed demeans a man, takes away his dignity. We have, and that includes you and me, to work on some way of re-organising society.

'It's fine being armchair politicians and deciding how the country should be run. What we have to do is to recognise the real problem, because it is not going to go away, and as a community, a county, a nation we have to tackle this problem, each of us trying to contribute. Perhaps we can look forward to the day when we only do two or three days work a week and the rest of our time is spent in leisure, whatever that means.'

I knew Steve spent every minute of his spare time digging

away at his garden. He once said, 'My salary's now big enough for me to be able to afford to be a farm labourer.'

'Steve,' I said, 'thanks for your advice. I shall vote for you as a future Prime Minister.'

Steve smiled.

'But me,' I said, 'how do I cope with all these people who come into the surgery: the depressed, redundant executive; the disturbed striker?'

'One of the most important things,' said Steve, 'and one of the most effective treatments is sitting patiently listening to people, whatever their troubles.'

'You mean a bit like the way you sit and listen to me?'

Steve smiled again.

'Yes,' he said. 'Something like that.'

CHAPTER 11

Changing Times

I was growing older. When I first came to Tadchester I had been completely involved in local affairs, playing for the rugby club until Steve Maxwell suggested that a two-legged partner might be more use than a one-legged one. I played cricket in the summer, went seine fishing off the beaches, and was part of the Round Table tableau in carnival processions.

I now had to leave the Round Table and move up into the 41 Club.

I became president of the rugby club instead of one of its players. I was on the carnival committee, vice-chairman of two cricket clubs and both the rowing clubs — offices which really meant that they came to me for subscriptions — medical officer for two or three horse shows a year, and deeply involved in Red Cross work.

As if life wasn't busy enough, I was asked a couple of times to stand for the council. I talked to old Billy Beer about it. He was a builder Up-the-Hill, with a family business that went back several generations.

'They asked me to stand several times,' said Billy. 'But I refused. Two or three of my builder friends were elected and the difference between them and me is that they went bankrupt and

I am still going. You've got to have plenty of spare time if you want to do council work properly.'

Tadchester had a tremendous depth of history. At one time it had been a major centre for the importation of tea into this country, and the old historic buildings in the town were jealously preserved and guarded. It was a town to be proud of.

The biggest danger to its identity came with the increasing numbers of holidaymakers who came pouring down every year. Holiday camps and caravan sites at Sanford-on-Sea grew and grew.

Broken-down cottages all over the countryside and in the small creeks and bays were steadily being bought up by people from the cities. A couple of new hotels were built, with sophisticated bars and dining rooms and large swimming pools. It was like a leap into the space age for Tadchester.

But in spite of these fairly obvious changes, the heart and strength of the town was little changed.

Many an entrepreneur came down to settle and thought he'd take over the town, get on the council, be mayor, but he would always come across the same rigid defences. There was only one certain way of getting elected to anything in Tadchester and that was to be a Methodist.

During the General Election at the end of the Second World War I was in South Yorkshire, working as a Bevin Boy down the coal mines. The locals said they would vote for a pig if it was Labour.

Here in Tadchester if you weren't a member of the Methodist Church, then it was pretty hard going. The only man ever to beat the Methodist stranglehold was an itinerant builder from Up-the-Hill who could neither read nor write, but he did have 630 relatives who all put their crosses on his ballot papers. It was typical of Tadchester that once elected, the illiterate councillor should be put in charge of choosing books for the library.

Tadchester Hospital had been built by the local community, taken over by the National Health, and was now being run down from an active hospital to a geriatric unit. All major cases were being referred to Winchcombe Hospital ten miles away.

When Henry retired, it was likely there would be no more surgery at Tadchester. It was rumoured that the Government were going to build a health centre in the grounds of the hospital and that we should vacate our surgery premises.

This was all in the name of progress but there was only one way out of Tadchester, across Tadchester Bridge on the Winchcombe Road, and in the summer this was a terrible bottle-neck. In June, July and August, if a woman was on her way to Winchcombe in labour, she had about a fifty-fifty chance of having her baby in the ambulance.

What midwifery facilities we had had in Tadchester had been withdrawn. The old St Mary's Maternity Home had been closed down. We missed it terribly. Home confinements got fewer and fewer and we had to accept the fact that we were losing our skills as obstetricians.

Strangely, the old St Mary's Maternity Home with its lack of hygiene — in fact a dog came and lifted its leg in the delivery unit when I was making my first delivery — never had any troubles with infection.

This small unit was probably overrun with the local germs of the local people. Now our young mothers had to go over to a big sterile unit in Winchcombe. Immediately there was an increase in various infections picked up by both mothers and babies.

My old friend, Bob Barker, at the bookshop, smiled when I complained about all these changes.

'It's part of an unending pattern, Bob,' he said. 'These are fashions. Big is beautiful and then small is beautiful, we can only really find out by trying. If we could learn by our mistakes each time we got some new project, then we might advance.

'The trouble is that when you have new brooms, changes are made for changes' sake. It's not always wise.

'By and large there are probably better medical services down here than when you first came. This has been at the expense of the personal, caring sort of medicine that was practised before.

'The next move will be for somebody to discover all sorts of disadvantages in medicine being de-personalised. There'll be

the great move back again to small units, until somebody decides that it is time that we had bigger units again. I've seen it all happen in every sphere of life.

'Everything goes round in circles. All the time we do edge forward, but not nearly as much as we think.'

He reached behind him for an old book which catalogued prices of goods on sale at an apothecary's in the seventeenth century.

I looked down through the lists. About half the things I recognised as still being in use today — senna, rhubarb, opium, isinglass — a few we didn't use — sea horse pizzle, crabs' eyes and a lovely sounding medicine called skink.

'What is skink?' said Bob Barker.

'I've no idea,' I said, 'but if it was available I'd certainly use it.'

'Now,' said Bob, 'you say about half the things on this list are still being used today. I wonder how many times they have been discovered and abandoned and re-discovered over the last three hundred years?'

I looked at them closely. I could think of a couple of items that had been picked up and discarded at least three times in my time in medicine.

'What you should do,' said Bob, 'in addition to having a go at writing, is to interest yourself in music and painting or even writing poetry. It's only in the arts that we can make any real advances, break new barriers, find new methods of communication.

'I don't mean to be disrespectful to the medical profession,' he said, 'but all you can do is get better at keeping people alive. I wonder if that on its own is enough.

'I remember the Roald Dahl story of the obstetrician who used all his skill to procure at last a live birth for a woman:

'"What are you going to call the baby, Mrs Hitler," he asked her.

'"Adolf," she replied.

'Perhaps,' he said, 'as we have more and more leisure time there will be more time to cross new barriers in the artistic world.

'We might even reach a stage where you would have to justify having some medical treatment,' he said with a grin. 'You are keeping us all alive so long nowadays we might reach a stage where to have your appendix out you might have to produce a certificate to say you are a worthwhile case.

'Thank goodness,' he said, 'I'll have gone before all these things happen.'

Steve Maxwell and Bob Barker have been a great influence on my life. Wise, kindly men, unselfish and almost without prejudice.

*   *   *

Pam and I were sitting on the balcony one day looking out over the estuary.

'What will happen,' I said, 'when Steve Maxwell and Bob Barker have gone? Nobody lasts for ever. Whom will I chat to then about the world and how to put it right?'

Pam said, 'Well, you'll be a bit older then. And the likelihood is that the ageing Dr Clifford will be one of the wise old men of the town, and it will be you who'll be offering tea and sympathy.'

'I can't ever see that happening,' I said.

'Oh come on, Peter Pan,' said Pam. 'Let's go off and have a swim.'

*   *   *

For some years it had been my ambition to write. I was encouraged to try by Bob Barker and by Joan Courage, a local author who took me to the Writers' Summer School in Derbyshire.

The writers at the school liked to have a doctor around. I was useful because I could clarify medical situations and plots, give details on how to poison somebody or how to perform an operation. There were questions such as when did anaesthetics first start to be used? Could I suggest how somebody could be killed in hospital by a visitor apart from being bored to death?

The first two scripts I wrote — both short stories based on courageous patients of mine — were accepted by the BBC. I broadcast both of them and was beginning to regard myself as an author and broadcaster of great talent. The BBC must have thought differently because they rejected the next twenty-seven scripts.

Pam had a friend who was about to do her first BBC recording of a script she had written. Was there any advice I could give her? With the experience of a full eight minutes on the air behind me, I was prepared to advise anybody. I gave the friend the benefit of my vast knowledge and asked if she would put her script on tape for me. This she did. The lady had the broadest Devon accent and all she did was talk about the pigs on her farm and the paying guests in the summer. It really was appalling — so I thought — but I kept my counsel.

While I was getting my twenty-seven rejections Pam's friend, Nancy Horner, was asked back again and again to do more and more recordings, and soon became an established radio personality. Though over the years I was to do many broadcasts for the BBC, I was never anywhere near as accomplished or successful as the fascinating lady I had first thought so appalling.

Tadchester rugby team asked me to write some first-aid instructions for them. I knew that these big, hairy rugby players would never look at normal first-aid instructions, so I decided to funny them up, to use the laughs to get the message across.

I finished up with enough for a small book, so I sent it off to a publisher. Like my first broadcast, it was accepted straightaway and I went up to London to meet the publisher.

I was ushered into a huge room. Sitting behind a vast mahogany desk was a man of about my own age, smart-suited, wearing executive glasses and smoking a huge cigar.

'Pleased to meet you, Dr Clifford,' he said. 'Congratulations on your book. I think it will do well.'

'Thank you,' I said. 'When is it likely to be published?'

'Monday, 17th September,' he said. 'We've chosen a Monday because on that day there is more space given to book reviews in the Press. After the weekend people read their papers more intently than any other day of the week. And we have found that books published on a Monday do better, by and large, than books published on any other day of the week.'

'Sounds great,' I said. 'But the 17th of September is a Thursday.'

The publisher did not bat an eyelid.

'Thursday,' he said, 'is a good day as well.'

He sounded exactly like a consultant physician.

I enjoyed my writing and broadcasting, attaining small successes but never achieving any great heights. It was a tremendous help to my medicine to have an outside interest and to meet such different groups of people.

Although I was never going to win the Pulitzer Prize, I had found something that I enjoyed doing, and which in some strange way held me steady for my main work of being a family doctor.

CHAPTER 12

Letter from America

An unexpected letter from America brought memories of student days flooding back. It was from Paul Young who had been one of my firm friends during that time.

Pre-clinical years, three in number if you get your exams at the right time, are some of the most frustrating years of medical training. Although nominally a medical student, you know nothing about medicine and any self-respecting ambulanceman or first aider could leave you way behind in the management of even minor accidents.

This did not deter a couple of fellow students in their first year (when their nearest approach to medicine had been the dissection of a dog fish) from offering their medical services. The inference that they were nearly doctors gave them introductions to all sorts of functions: football matches, boxing matches and even some expeditions. They would tackle everything, nipping back to read a book on the management of casualties between cases. Providing they followed what they read, all was well.

Being a first-year medical student as opposed to a schoolboy you could wander around with the hospital scarf thrown nonchalantly round your neck, drop into pubs at lunchtime and revel in the fact that you were an embryo doctor.

Then came the second-year slog. Corpses that had soaked in formalin bore no relation to anybody you knew. Dissection, which implies bold strokes with a knife, was in fact scratching through grubby plasticine-like tissue trying to identify nerves, arteries, muscles and bones which were nothing like the beautiful pictures in text books.

We were taught some medical testing, prefaced by a classic,

lecturer's trick. A jar of urine was placed in front of us. The lecturer announced that a crude test for diabetes was whether or not you could taste the sugar in urine. He then pushed his finger into the urine, put it in his mouth, and said he wasn't sure about this particular sample.

Three or four 'volunteers' were asked to come up and repeat this procedure. They all pulled funny faces, one of them was sick and none of them could decide whether there was any sugar in the urine or not.

'The main thing I am teaching you here is observation — the single most important thing in medicine,' said the lecturer. 'If you had looked closely you would have noticed that it was my index finger that I placed in the jar and it was the third finger that I put into my mouth.'

Paul Young was an American. He was a six-foot, thirteen-stone American football player who had come to England after having taken an organic chemistry degree at an American university. He was on a scholarship and intended to go back to America with an English degree in medicine.

He was also anxious to enjoy every minute of his stay in England and absorb much of its culture. He would have a go at anything; he played rugby enthusiastically and got himself a place in the hospital second team on the wing. His loudly shouted American football terms were a great asset although often confusing, not only for the opponents but also for his own side.

He was a beaver for work and put us all to shame. He wore a large pair of horn-rimmed spectacles and was usually seen carrying great tomes under his arm. He was always eager to get into discussion about the various work projects we were involved on. He asked endless questions in lectures without causing irritation.

Anatomy and physiology are never really a test of one's ability; they are much more a test of application, stamina and determination and one just had to sit down and solidly learn things. There Paul Young had the advantage over us. If given an area of textbook to cover, he could quickly commit it to memory and could recall it almost word for word. In fact, he could sometimes recite two or three whole pages of text.

But for some reason he didn't do terribly well when we had our terminal examinations. He came in the top third in the organic chemistry examination at the end of the first year but didn't do as well as expected of a man with a degree in this subject. He was well liked by all the lecturers and it was quite obvious he knew his stuff. They did their best to explain to him that he was answering questions in the wrong way and it wasn't a lack of ability that was getting him such low marks.

During the last three months before the final pre-clinical examinations you have to memorise so much information. There is very little to be worked out, one simply has to amass the detailed knowledge of the body and its workings which will be the basis on which you build your medical career and which must last you for the rest of your life. We were obviously well taught, for even thirty years after qualifying, odd bits of anatomy that I thought I had forgotten come into mind when required.

We were all nervously entered for our second medical examination; you were nothing until you had passed second M.B. In Oxford and Cambridge you get a degree for second M.B., in London you get nothing. Once you have passed your second M.B. then you are certain to qualify eventually for a degree of some sort or another that will enable you to practise medicine.

Paul had worked at least as hard as any of us and, looking at our group, if anybody had to put a bet on who would pass highest in the rankings, it would be Paul. And yet he got the lowest marks in anatomy ever recorded, which absolutely shattered him.

I hadn't expected to pass. I hadn't worked hard, had played a lot of rugby and was secretary of the rugby fifteen. I hadn't really prepared myself. You have another chance in the summer and I wrote off the summer to swotting hard for the second M.B., which that time I got.

Paul failed again, and I gathered that his second attempt was only slightly better than his first.

It certainly wasn't exam nerves, and it certainly wasn't a lack of ability or application. The main reason must have been some difference in the way we are examined in this country as opposed to the United States. It is not that our system is better or that we have a higher standard: it's just in some way different.

Paul was at least as well informed as any of us, and better than most. He understood what he was doing, had a good grasp of everything, was able and intellectual, but somehow he could not come to terms with the British examinations. He returned to America, settled back into medical school there, passed all his degrees with honours, specialised in paediatrics and became a well-known paediatrician.

Although we didn't see each other after he left for America, we kept in touch and a letter from him saying that he was coming to London on a post-graduate course meant that Pam and I would travel to London to stay with my mother and have a few days with him.

Paul was in a party of six, his wife and two other Americans and their wives, all delightful charming people. They were mixing their morning lectures with various London entertainments. They were determined to absorb as much of London culture as they could, and were going to a matinee every afternoon, the theatre in the evening and sometimes a late-night film as well. What suckers they were for punishment.

Paul had changed very little: he was slightly stouter, still wore thick horn-rimmed glasses, was as friendly as ever, and more British than the British. His wife was a very striking dark-haired woman called Peggy. She was extremely smartly dressed and came from one of the great Californian wine families. Like myself, she had an interest in writing.

We took them as our guests to see our friend Joan Miller in the 'Three Ladies' starring Dame Flora Robson, and Peter Cotes, Joan's husband, entertained them all after the show. They were delighted to be in the presence of such famous English stage people.

Their stay went all too quickly and almost before we had realised it, it was their last night here.

They wanted to take us out somewhere, and after careful

planning they decided to treat us to a meal in a hotel which specialised in the re-creation of the Elizabethan scene. As they didn't know where the hotel was, I, as the only Englishman and part-time Londoner, was elected to select our mode of transport to the site of this repast.

After careful enquiries I managed to find a bus which unfortunately dropped us off over a mile from the hotel, leaving us to complete the journey on foot. I explained that, medically, exercise was the best thing for us, especially in view of the volume of food we were about to consume, but there was little enthusiasm from the rest of the party.

We arrived at our destination late, to be ushered into a candlelit room by a number of wenches who characterised the age by having the top half of their bosoms exposed. If you are interested in bosoms, as I am, it is worth going for that alone.

Being the last in we had to sit at the top table (the only one vacant) and our host, Paul, had to sit in the grand armchair as lord and master, whilst Pam, who sat on his right, was informed that she was his mistress for the night. On enquiring tenatively about her duties, to her relief she found that she was required only to put food on his plate.

We were above the salt, i.e. the landlords, which meant that we had the right to collect taxes from the people who were seated below the salt, and didn't have to pay taxes ourselves. I immediately determined to visit my local income tax office the next day and explain my change of status. The demarcation line was a large box of salt at the end of our table, forming a barrier to the next one.

We started with a mead aperitif, followed by a mulled wine which (to my distrusting palate) had some Spanish ancestry. We had instructions to greet each other by shouting something like 'Hail, Wassail!', which is apparently Elizabethan for 'Bottoms up'. I shouted 'Seig heil!' all the time and nobody appeared to notice. (It was so much easier to say.)

The tables in front of us were filled with lively Americans from a special 'Three-Week Five-Country Tour'. Owing to my travel arrangements, they had a head start on us and were already busy drinking and wassailing when we arrived. This was their second meal in three nights at this establishment, and being the last night of their tour, they were determined to go back to their mother country having experienced a bit of Old England or bust in the effort. (Nothing to do with the wenches.)

The chief wench, who also happened to have the largest bust (probably this is an example of natural selection), was trying to describe medieval customs but had to shout above the surrounding din. We discovered that 'If you didn't leave some of your hog's head salad for your beef, you were fined,' and 'If you were on a lower table and wanted salt, you were dependent on the whim of the lord and master.' Meanwhile an attractive green-clad singer was plucking her guitar (or Elizabethan equivalent) and singing Elizabethan ballads. As the Three-Week Five-Country Tour rapidly lost their inhibitions, her music disappeared amongst cries of 'A drink for Milwaukee . . . now one for Kansas City!'

Meanwhile we were served with our first course: soup; and in true Elizabethan style had to drink it straight from the bowl. We had a quick international discussion and found that all children of our party, both British and American, drank their soup in this way, and we decided that this must be some sort of infantile subconscious recognition that Elizabeth II was on the throne.

Next hog's head and salad.

The food was good and the wine, if I questioned its origin, was available in abundant quantities.

It was leading to the complete disintegration of the Three-Week Five-Country Tour in front of us. Everybody in this party was embracing everybody else, and one group of women with the experience of five countries behind them, had started to tackle a group of British businessmen who had unwisely entered this un-native scene. Soon the wine began to act on them too, and they proceeded to match the embraces of the American Amazons, one for one.

One girl in a bright-red frock stuck loyally to her own party and began to 'eat' in the most vigorous manner a thick-set man with a hairline moustache, sitting next to her. One older lady of

the party, with a high nasal whine, turned and said, 'That girl had the worse luck of the trip. She lost her bags [presumably cases] in Amsterdam and her passport in Paris.' I hated to think what she was likely to lose tonight, but suggested she would be able to put in her diary, 'The night my luck changed.'

Paul managed to rescue the minstrel and we grouped to form a protective ring about her while she sang us some delightful Elizabethan ditties. Some had exactly the same music as well-known rugby songs, thus dispelling the legend that this game started when Tom Brown, at Rugby School, picked up the ball and ran. I'd always thought, when I saw pictures of Sir Walter Raleigh, that he looked rather like a scrum-half.

The Three-Week Five-Country Tour were getting quite

worked up now and a few of the wenches who moved in to keep the party clean probably gave the impression to later diners that bruised bosoms were the fashion round about the time of the Armada.

Then suddenly 'Auld Lang Syne', and the party was over, and everybody went quietly home (though I did see one man and a wench slipping upstairs and wondered if she was going to show him an old Elizabethan bed).

It had been a great evening. I told Paul I was grateful to him, for at last I had found out about my own heritage.

We promised to go and see Paul and his wife in the States, and it was pleasant to know that this delightful man, who somehow did not fit into the British examination system, had prospered in the different academic climate of America.

CHAPTER 13

Diets and Boat Trips

We very much enjoyed our house, which was sited on three-quarters of an acre of wooded garden overlooking the estuary.

I could watch salmon boats rowing up the river and herons fishing from its banks, and could see Tadchester's two fishing trawlers coming home on the incoming tide with their following flocks of gulls.

Far away, across the other side of the river, was the main road to Winchcombe. The seasons could be noted by the volume of traffic on this road, a much better guide than the unstable British weather.

Since Pam lost her mother, her father Gerry had become

increasingly despondent. He had had an unsuccessful attempt to set up house with a musical housekeeper — part of her job was to play piano accompaniment to his violin — and they talked of buying a property near us. Finally he built a bungalow extension to our house, and it gave him an even better view of the estuary and river than we had.

Food was a very important part of Gerry's life. He could smell a mile off if we had anything special cooking and was very hurt if he wasn't asked to any dinner party that was going. At Christmas he hovered round to see that his trifle with hazelnuts on it was prepared in the way that he liked it (he didn't like Christmas pudding). When, on a visit, my mother offered him some bacon and egg pie, he was quite affronted: he considered that food for peasants. Only the very best for Gerry.

'To keep fit,' he said, 'you've got to have a well-balanced diet. You ought to know that, Bob m'lad.'

I was never quite sure what a well-balanced diet was and always failed to persuade Pam that there was probably as much nourishment in a glass of milk and a ham salad sandwich as there was in roast beef and Yorkshire pudding.

One of the fittest men locally was Trevor Robinson, a confirmed bachelor — not that he did not like women, he liked them so much he could never settle on any particular one.

A great keep-fit enthusiast, he rowed and played squash, badminton and cricket. Although forty-seven, in temperament and outlook he was really only in his middle-twenties. He drank like a fish, often stayed up all night drinking and playing cards, but never seemed to be tired. He was always in demand for local hospital functions. Having an eligible bachelor like Trevor as make-weight for the many nurses who were without partners was invaluable and every new woman who met him felt that she might be the one to break down his barriers.

Pam and I had been to one particularly late-night dance and staggered home about two o'clock in the morning. We were aroused about ten o'clock by the noise of motorboats racing up and down the river. I peered through the window to see Trevor Robinson water-skiing.

We had left him at two o'clock with the party in full swing. I doubt if he had been in bed before five and, knowing Trevor, probably not alone. I waved to him from our balcony as he came back up the river and he slipped his rope, glided to the bank, pulled off his water-skis and walked up to our house for coffee. 'Good God, Trevor,' I said. 'How on earth do you manage it?'

'Diet,' he said. 'Purely diet. Apart from the odd time I dine out or am invited for a meal, I only eat two things — tinned salmon and pineapple chunks.'

'Isn't that expensive?' I said, only half believing him.

'No,' he said. 'I get them all free.'

Trevor was the senior sales rep for a canned foods firm and it was a perk of the job that salesmen were able to keep goods damaged in transit. I gathered that most of the salesmen in his firm fed themselves for nothing. When their supplies were dwindling, a packer could very easily be persuaded to drop a case accidentally.

Trevor one day showed me his larder — and he hadn't been joking. The whole of the left side of the pantry was stacked with tinned salmon and the other side with pineapple chunks. All, of course, with dents in them.

'Don't you ever get bored?'

'No,' said the ebullient Trevor, 'I love them both.'

I have no idea what magic ingredients tinned salmon and pineapple chunks possess to ensure a well-balanced diet. I know Trevor reinforced this basic minimum with plenty of beer.

When he was away from home, he must have eaten normally. He specialised in holidays abroad and would bring back colourful slides from far-off places such as Thailand, Morocco and South America. He used to give talks about his travels to all the various bodies in the town — Rotarians, Round Table, Women's Institutes — and then after drinks in the Tadchester Arms, you would hear the unabridged version of his exploits in Thailand massage parlours and South American brothels. He was a great laugh, was Trevor. I never knew if the stories he told us were true but they were very entertaining. Perhaps his brief intakes of foreign food balanced his tinned diet, anyway it worked.

* * *

Gerry tried to get involved in as many local sporting activities as he could. He was a good shot, he fished a bit and played very mediocre golf. Music was his real love. He had been a very good violinist and now played in orchestras for the local operatic societies and was a member of various trios and quartets whose playing sounded absolutely ghastly to me, but it obviously gave all the participants great pleasure.

We had a small dinghy with an outboard motor. A nice boat, but it had its limitations. It wasn't really big enough to go out to sea for a start. When we took it out on the river the tide had to be right, otherwise several hundred yards of sticky mud had to be traversed; also the weather had to be right; and I had to be off duty to supervise the children.

Gerry came into our house for coffee one Saturday morning and we looked out over the estuary together. He pointed to our small boat, rocking gently at its mooring.

'You could do with a bigger boat,' he said. 'With a 25-foot clinker-built job and an inboard motor we could do a bit of deep-sea fishing. I fancy my hand at that.'

Gerry was now seventy-six and I thought this was a bit old for taking up deep-sea fishing. But he had successfully taken up camping at the age of seventy-five so nothing was impossible.

'Chap's written to me,' said Gerry, 'saying he's got a 25-foot clinker-built boat with an inboard, lying at Abersoch in North Wales.' (What a coincidence.) 'If we'd like to have it brought down we can have it for nothing.'

'You're not going to sail it down?' I said.

'Good God, no,' said Gerry. 'We'll have it brought down by trailer.'

'That's fine,' I said. 'Shall we fix it up?'

'Better have a look at it,' said Gerry. 'What about going up on your next weekend off?'

It was February now. We were down on the Somerset coast. I didn't fancy driving up to Wales overnight. In the end, Gerry persuaded me and one Friday night we set off.

It was bitterly cold. The car didn't have a heater and the windscreen wipers weren't working quite as they should. The further north we went, the colder it got. I was driving Gerry's car, a Morris Minor Traveller, which was slightly better than mine.

Dawn was breaking about fifty miles north of Bristol when we came across an accident. A little A30 bubble car had driven into the rear of a lorry, and the scene was quite appalling. The lorry driver and his mate had pulled out the driver of the A30, who was sitting at the side of the road with blood streaming down his face. The lorry driver and his chum were standing near the cab talking away as if nothing was amiss.

I pulled up and asked, 'What happened?'

'He's crashed into the back of our lorry, mate,' said the driver.

'Have you sent for an ambulance?' I asked.

'No,' he said, 'there's nowhere to phone from.'

We were way out in the country.

'What are you doing?'

'Waiting for a passing car.'

'Well, has anything passed?'

He said, 'You have. Do you know any first aid?'

'I'm a doctor.'

'Good, I'll leave it to you, mate,' he said.

The injured man was sitting holding his head in his hands, blood running through his fingers. He was an awful sight.

His car had run under the extended tailboard of the lorry, smashing his spectacles and putting glass into both eyes.

'I think I'm blind,' he said.

'We'd better take him to the nearest town,' I said. I knew that Netherton was only ten miles off and should have some sort of hospital.

We managed to get him into the back of our Traveller, wrapped him up in a blanket and drove off towards Netherton.

We found a cottage hospital with a rather diffident sister on duty.

'What can we do for you at this hour?' she said.

'There's been a road accident,' I replied. 'This man's eyes are badly damaged.'

'I don't know if we can get a doctor at this time of day,' she said, 'but you'd better bring him in.'

We brought him in and sat him down. His face was still bloody and he was in obvious pain.

'Hm,' said the sister, 'I expect I'd better ring the doctor. He won't like to be disturbed at a time like this.'

She went off to the phone. 'He's in his bath,' she said. 'He'll come when he's finished.'

Gerry had noticed as we drove into the hospital that the police station was only just up the road.

'I'll walk up,' he said, 'and report the accident.'

He came back ten minutes later looking exasperated.

'How did you get on, Gerry?' I asked.

'Well,' he said, 'I went up there and there was a chap digging in the garden of the police station. I went up to the police station and knocked on the door. There was no reply. I knocked again. There was no reply so I said to the chap in the garden, who'd been watching me all this time, "Do you know where the policeman is?"

'"Yes," he said, "I'm him — but it's no good talking to me: I'm off duty. You'll have to go and ring up the station in the next town."'

Gerry was fuming.

'May I use your phone?' he asked the sister.

'Why?' she said, looking suspicious.

'I must phone and report this accident,' said Gerry as patiently as he could.

'Oh, all right,' said the sister.

Gerry rang the police sation in the next town. 'I want to report an accident,' he said.

'What's your name?' said the voice at the other end.

'Never mind my name,' said Gerry, 'I want to report an accident.'

'What's your name?' said the voice at the other end.

'I'm not involved in the accident,' said Gerry. 'We just happened to have helped somebody involved in it.'

'What's your name?' said the man at the other end.

Gerry gave a description of the accident and slammed the phone down.

The casualty sister came up to him.

'That's sixpence for your phone call,' she said.

Gerry was getting redder and redder in the face.

'Where's the bloody doctor?' he said.

'We won't have that language in here,' said the sister. 'This is only a cottage hospital and he's on call. It is very good of him to come at all.'

I was getting a bit impatient too by now.

'Look,' I said, 'this man's got glass in his eyes. Can I be doing something?'

'Hm,' said the sister. Realising the man was in a bad way, she volunteered to give the doctor another ring.

We'd been at the hospital an hour by then. The sister came back. 'The doctor will be here in half an hour,' she said, 'he's just having his breakfast. He says if you do feel you can do something, he would be very grateful.'

I cleaned up the chap's eyes as best I could, bandaged them to protect them from the light, gave him something to ease his pain and saw him settled down in the ward.

'Come on, Gerry,' I said, 'we're off. There's nothing more we can do here.'

We set off in the car. It had now begun to snow. We had to call in on Gerry's friend who was donating the boat and it meant a diversion through the Llangollen Pass.

In the Pass it had obviously been snowing for a long time. We crept along in blinding snow over treacherous roads and eventually reached his friend's house.

'They'll give us a bloody good breakfast here,' said Gerry, smacking his hands together.

We arrived at nine o'clock and were obviously very unpopular. The man hadn't told his wife we were coming for breakfast. We were shown into a cold dining room, where we sat shivering until eventually we were reluctantly brought some tea and toast and given directions how to get to the boat at Abersoch. We set off on our way again.

The car was bitterly cold, the road was very difficult to drive, Gerry hadn't had the breakfast he had expected, the windscreen wipers had frozen almost to a stop — and then suddenly the car slid gently into a ditch.

It wouldn't budge. The wheels just spun and it was too heavy to push.

'Christ,' said Gerry, who had been getting steadily more irritable. 'What else can happen today?'

After about half an hour a tractor came along the road. It stopped near us and a bewhiskered farmer got off.

'You're in trouble,' he said, perceptively.

'Can you help us?' I asked.

'I don't know,' he said. 'I'm not really licensed to do this sort of thing. Don't think I can, really.'

I put my hand into my trouser pocket and saw his face brighten. I extracted two pounds from my wallet.

'Will this help?'

'Have you out in a jiffy, sir,' he said. A rope from the back of the tractor tugged us out of the ditch and we were on our creepy crawl again.

As we got nearer to Abersoch the weather and the road got better. The sun gave a sort of wintry smile and after numerous enquiries, we found a little cove. There, covered by a tarpaulin, was the boat we'd come to look at.

'It's been worth it,' said Gerry. 'Look at it.'

She certainly was a beauty, with sturdy but graceful lines. I could already imagine us riding the waves as we went out to Tadchester bay. This was just the boat for a fisherman like me.

Gerry reached into his pocket for a penknife and stuck it into the nearest planking.

'Bloody rotten,' he said. 'It's no good. It's a wasted journey.'

Both sides of the boat had areas of rotting timbers. Though it looked good from a distance, the craft was complete rubbish. We would have been doing Gerry's friend a favour by taking it away.

'Come on,' I said. 'Home we go.'

It was late afternoon and we had had just about enough. We decided to stay for the night in Criccieth.

Gerry was very disgruntled by now. 'Bet the food'll be bloody awful,' he said.

The hotel was quite comfortable. There was a big log fire and Gerry improved as he sat with a glass of whisky, toasting his feet in front of the roaring logs.

'By God,' he said, 'I could eat a horse.'

The food was simple fare but not at all bad: a great big bowl of oxtail soup, roast beef, Yorkshire pudding and roast potatoes with great mounds of soggy cabbage.

Gerry packed food in like a man stoking a raging furnace. He smacked his lips as he pushed away his empty plate.

'Now for something tasty,' he said, 'just to finish it off. What have you got, Miss?' he asked the fat, pimply waitress in the grubby white pinafore.

'Well,' she said, 'there's some prunes and custard, semolina pudding or you could have a bit of Stilton.'

'God,' said Gerry, 'I don't want semolina or prunes. I'll have to settle for the Stilton.

'I expect it'll be a little bit of dried-up stuff,' he moaned. 'What a bloody waste of a journey. All these miles... the windscreen wipers don't work... I'll have to have the car serviced... blood all over the back of the car... frozen...' but then his face suddenly lit up. Across the dining room came our dumpy waitress almost staggering under the weight of a huge half Stilton.

'My God,' said Gerry. 'This is perfect.'

A large glass of port, a great wooden spoon, a pile of biscuits, and butter — Gerry was in business.

'Not such a bad trip after all,' he said, munching away. 'I feel like a man restored. The best bit of cheese I've had for years. Now then, what are we going to order for breakfast?'

Gerry's port and Stilton had certainly revived him. I was still exhausted. We'd missed a night's sleep, been cold and wet, I had been driving a strange car, we had come all this way for nothing and I felt low and exhausted.

'Come on, Bob,' said Gerry, 'I see they've got kidneys. Not often you get kidneys offered for breakfast.'

'Well, if you insist,' I said, 'but I'd rather have some tinned salmon and pineapple chunks.'

They were the only things I could think of that might give me sufficient energy to make the journey home.

CHAPTER 14

First Pike

I had fixed up to have a day off on October 1st to go fishing for pike with John Denton.

'Why wait till then?' I asked, having seen several pike brought into the Tadchester Arms during the summer.

'Tradition,' said John. 'On some waters you're not allowed to fish for pike at all until October 1st. This river authority doesn't like pike, so people are allowed to catch them all through the coarse season. But October 1st is the accepted date. Worth waiting for: gives you more a sense of occasion.'

Although the Tad was a mixed fishery, it held a good head of trout, topped up by John's re-stocking every year. The trout fishermen certainly hated pike. They claimed that they played havoc with the stocks, and they kept up a strong lobby with the river authority to have the numbers kept down.

'Pike do knock off a number of trout,' said John. 'But in the main, trout can look after themselves better than most. And if I know a particular pike's doing a lot of damage, I'll soon have him out.

'But what the pike do is to keep the river healthy, keep the head of fish in balance with the food supply. Take all the pike out and you'd end up with a water full of stunted, sickly fish.

'That's one thing pike do: see off the sick fish. They're bone idle by nature and only hunt in short sprints. So any fish which is off-colour and slowing down a bit makes an ideal target.'

'Vicious-looking things, aren't they?' I said, remembering the monster in the glass case above the bar at the Tadchester Arms.

'They are,' said John. 'Freshwater shark, they're often called. And that's another reason they're treated so badly — they frighten people.'

I found out how much they frightened people on the morning of October 1st. John and I were walking along the bank towards the chosen swim, when we saw a man booting something through the grass. He kicked it some distance away from the water, then stamped on it hard three or four times.

'Hey up,' said John. 'If this is what I think it is...'

The man was short, bespectacled, balding, middle-aged, with a round face which, as we discovered later, was normally quite pleasant. A typical family man out for a day by the river. He was filling his pipe as we reached him, and looking at the thing in the grass. He was trembling quite noticeably.

'By the...' he panted, his eyes wide and triumphant. 'Took some putting down, that one. Thought it was going to have my hand off.'

'That one' was a pike. Badly mangled from the kicking and stamping, still quivering but very dead.

John took a tape measure from his pocket and ran it down the length of the fish.

'Know what length this is?' he asked coldly.

'Ooh... Three feet if it's an inch,' said the little man, his trembling subsiding as he drew on his pipe.

'It's 23 inches long,' said John. 'Which gives it a weight of 3½ lb. And 23 inches is an inch under the minimum length. That fish should have been returned to the water straightaway. Unharmed.'

'Get away,' said the man. 'I nearly lost my fingers with that thing. Who the hell are you, anyway?'

'That's me,' said John, producing his bailiff's identification card. 'Now then, I could have you banned for a season for what you've just done. Taking an undersized fish for a start. And kicking the bloody thing to death for a second.'

'I'm sorry,' the little man stuttered. 'I didn't know...'

'Well you know now,' said John. 'If I ever catch you doing it again, that's your fishing up the spout for a while. Now get back to that water and try for another. When you've got one on, give me a shout — I'll only be round that bend — and I'll show you how a pike should be treated. Right?'

'Right,' said the man, flushing with relief. 'Thank you.... Thanks very much.... Most grateful.... Thanks...'

'Thank me by behaving yourself in future. Now off you go...'

John and I went round the bend in the river to a spot facing a small spring which trickled into the river down the opposite bank.

He kitted me out with a 10-foot, hollow fibreglass rod — which I found out later was really designed for carp fishing — and baited up with a dead and very smelly fish. The fish, a sprat heavily soaked in pilchard oil, was attached to the line with a single and a treble hook on a wire trace under a long, thick float.

'Get it over there, Bob,' he said. 'Just where that water's trickling in, downstream of that fallen log. There's a slow eddy there: just what the old pike likes.'

I cast in, the bait sank, the float righted itself, and I reeled in the slack line.

'Right,' said John. 'Keep your eyes on the float. You'll soon know when a pike takes the bait.

'For a start, let it run. It won't go far. The pike will stop to turn the bait in its mouth — it takes it sideways and swallows it head first — and then it will run again. On that second run, give it the hammer. Tighten up your line, stand up and strike firmly and smoothly. Nothing to it.'

We sat there for an hour, talking about this and that, but mainly pike.

'What was wrong with that man?' I asked. 'He seemed to be in a state of shock.'

'He was,' said John. 'Pike bring out the worst in people. All the buried frustrations, fears, aggressions, you name it. When a man catches a pike, all those complexes can explode.'

'But it's only a fish.'

'True. But weight-for-length it's a big one, and the most evil-looking we've got in this country. Mouth like a bear trap, lined with hundreds of needle-sharp teeth. All pointing backwards.

156

What goes in never comes out. But the biggest fright comes from the eyes.'

'Really evil, are they?'

'Not so much that as the fact they look straight at you. A pike needs binocular vision for hunting, so the eyes point straight ahead, not sideways as in other fish. The eyes, actually, are quite beautiful. T. H. White once said . . .'

Just then there was a loud yell from round the bend.

'T. H. White will have to wait,' said John. 'Me laddo's got himself a fish by the sound of it.'

He got up and moved off with long strides, keeping low so as not to disturb the fish in our stretch, putting his big feet down quietly. Leaving me staring at my float.

I am particularly prone to Sod's Law, and this time was no exception. Hardly had John disappeared than my float did the same. It shot underwater as if it had been snatched and moved swiftly upstream. Then it stopped and bobbed to the surface again.

Frantically willing myself not to panic, I waited for what seemed an age. The float waggled and bobbed and jiggled, and then slid firmly under, curving back downstream. I reeled in the slack line, stood up and struck with a long, firm, copybook strike over the right shoulder.

Thank God for the carp rod. Its flexible action absorbed the shock of the hooks going into what appeared to be a rock. Damn. It was snagged. I held tight to the rod for a second to work out how best to free the hook, then — *bang*!

There was a fierce tug on the line and the rod started to buck like a wild thing. The line thrummed with a jagging, side-to-side movement that pulled the rod tip almost down to the water. Remembering John's previous fishing lessons, I let out a little line, then turned the rod sideways to put sidestrain on whatever was threatening to drag me into the water.

The line went slack as the thing turned back upstream and I reeled frantically to make contact again. As soon as it tightened . . . *whoosh*! An enormous shape, like a blunt-headed torpedo, leapt clean out of the water, the tail thrashing the surface and the great head shaking from side to side in an attempt to throw the hooks.

With a great splash the fish belly-flopped onto the water and set off for another run, whipping the rod violently through the whole of its length. Some more line out, some more sidestrain and . . . *whoosh*! Out came the thing again, skittering upright on its tail across the surface, with the great mouth agape and the head shaking like a terrier with a rat.

'John!' I shouted, or tried to. What came out was a high-pitched squeak.

'What are you, Clifford? A man or a mouse?' I thought. Ignoring the answer of 'Pass the cheese', I followed the thing through as it crashed once more into the water, and this time dealt with the run a bit more calmly.

The fight seemed to go on for hours. Run after run and leap after leap, always with the same spectacular thrashing and head-shaking.

Another run. Here we go ag . . . But this time there was no leap. The pike ran frantically back and forth across the eddy, jagging all the time but now perceptibly weaker.

This was it. The Moment of Truth. John had taught me never to fight a fish to the point of complete exhaustion just for the fun of it. It was time to bring this thing across the river and net it. Thank God, too, for another of John's basic angling-for-idiots instructions: always make up the landing net before you start to fish. With this thing on the line, I could never have coped with screwing the net into the handle.

I started to pump the fish across, lifting the rod tip and then dropping it, reeling in the slack line every time. Got you now, me proud beauty. Another couple of . . . *whoosh*! A monstrous shape rocketed out of the water near the bank in a last desperate skittering bid for freedom, and so close now that I was splashed by its re-entry.

Right. Contact made again. One more pump. Net in water. Rod up slowly. Firmly draw the fish. *Eek*!

What faced me was a primaeval nightmare. A huge, scoop-shaped head. A mouth glittering silver with hundreds of tiny, vicious teeth. And a pair of immense eyes which accused me of every sin committed since the beginning of time.

My knees turned rubbery and my stomach cold and knotted. What the hell was I to *do* with this thing?'

'Hang on, Bob! I'm coming!' John's voice from a distant planet.

I couldn't lose it now. Not in front of witnesses. With a silent prayer and a firm grip, I drew the apparition over the submerged net. Such was its length that its snout was over the nearside rim of the net before its tail had touched the far one. Now or never — *hup*!

The fish thrashed, doubled up like a U-bend into the capacious mesh. I ran crabwise up the bank and at a safe distance from the water swung the net onto the grass with a scything movement which made sure the fish was covered by the mesh. I leaned hard on the net's rim. What on earth do I do now?

'Good lad, our Bob,' said John, kneeling beside me and pulling on a pair of thick leather gloves. 'I'll see to this — unless you fancy a go yourself.'

'No thanks, John,' I panted. 'He's all yours.'

John gingerly parted the mesh until the fish's great head was free. With his left hand John gripped the fish by the bony sockets behind the eyes. His right hand held a pair of long surgical forceps. Forcing the pike's mouth open with his knuckles, he probed into the great cavern and, with a couple of expert twists, freed the hooks.

(I discovered later that it was not uncommon for unenlightened anglers actually to stick finger and thumb into the eyes, blinding the pike while they forced in a cruel gag to hold the mouth open.)

'Nice one,' breathed John, taking the pike from the net and holding it down firmly on the grass. 'Tape measure in my right-hand pocket, Bob. Run it from the nose to the fork in the tail.'

This I did, warily. 'My God! Three foot one. Must weigh a ton.'

'Fifteen and a half pounds,' said John. 'Bloody good going by any standards.'

'What size do these things run to?'

'English record, about 37½ lb.' (That year it was to become 40 lb and is even more now). 'Scotland, nearly 48 lb; Ireland, 53 lb.'

'Sheesh! Makes mine look a bit sick.'

'Nay,' said John. 'That's a good 'un. You did well to hold him.'

'My, my,' said a voice behind me, almost repeating my words. 'That makes my little ones look a bit sick.'

It was the pike basher from round the bend. Now, seemingly, a reformed character.

After letting me admire the pike for a bit, John picked it up and laid it gently back in the water, head facing upstream. He held it for a minute or two, 'walking' it against the current to get the oxygenated water flowing over its gills, and with a final shove gave it its freedom. After a couple of confused shakes, it found its bearings and dived deep out of sight.

'I'm grateful to John here,' said the pleasant-faced little man. ('John' already. They must have got on well.) 'He took all the fright out of that second pike of mine. A five-pounder it was, too. What was that bit from T. H. White, John? You'd just started to tell me when your friend here screamed.'

Screamed?

'Ah, yes,' said John. 'My favourite quote about the pike. From *The Once and Future King* by T. H. White. You probably know it, Bob; where the future King Arthur, swimming in the moat after he'd been changed by Merlin into a fish, came across the old, giant pike.'

'Er, no. I can't say I do...'

'Sadness,' said John. 'That's what the pike's eyes hold if you look closely enough. And once you've recognised it, you'll never bash a pike again as long as you live. This is it...'

John intoned slowly and carefully, as if he were in a pulpit:

'"He was remorseless, disillusioned, predatory, fierce, pitiless — but his great jewel of an eye was that of a stricken deer, large, fearful, sensitive and full of griefs. He made no movement but looked upon them with his bitter eye."'

For a few seconds I was unable to speak. Those beautiful words, coming from this big, bluff man who would normally deny any pretensions to culture, spoken in a magical riverside setting with the murmur of the water as a background, were almost too much.

'Ahem,' I coughed, finally. 'That says it all, John. But I didn't know you were a literary man.'

'Nor I am,' said John. 'But T. H. White is special. Tells a good tale, that lad . . .'

CHAPTER 15

Leaving the Nest

My schooldays weren't the happiest days of my life, in fact some of them were very unhappy. I didn't do well in my early years at school neither distinguishing myself at work nor at games. It was only in my final years, when I started to apply myself, that I got any real sort of satisfaction and had any fun. As a result, I was determined that my children should enjoy their schooldays.

Pam and I had to decide whether or not to send the boys away to boarding school. Practically all my colleagues nearly ruined themselves sending their children to public school, really so that their children in turn would be in a position to nearly ruin themselves sending their own children to public school.

We decided that if there was adequate education locally, we would keep ours at home, perhaps selfishly, because we wanted to enjoy them and be involved in their growing up. We did have the advantage of living in a lovely area as part of a community

162

with plenty of local amenities and satisfactory local schools.

Having the children at home meant that we could support them in all the various functions they took part in. We became (I reluctantly) members of the Parents' and Teachers' Association and other such organisations.

If we supported one child in a particular activity we really had to support the others. We saw Jane at the age of four and a half tottering onto the stage with acute tonsilitis to say her bit as Noddy in a school play. We saw the disgruntled Paul in the school pantomime. Trevor and all Paul's friends were soldiers. Paul, to his disgust, was a dicky-bird. Zara made him the most superb bird costume, all fluffy blue feathers and a big yellow beak. Paul was outstanding in that; out of twenty birds, he was the only one with his beak pulled down over his left eye.

We sat right through one tedious play at the grammar school in which Trevor was to blow his trumpet. Having watched this badly acted, badly produced and badly directed play for three hours we were rewarded with our son's prowess — he came on at the last minute to blow a single note.

I have an open mind about religion and feel it's best for each to find his own way. Both Paul and Trevor became choirboys which meant that they attended church not for the religious service, but to perform as singers. They were thus exposed to religion but could make up their own minds whether they wanted to accept it or not.

School sports days could not be missed: Jane, grim and determined, always came in the first few; Trevor, good natured and determined, always came last but never minded; Paul, nervous and agitated, was never satisfied with less than first.

There were school concerts, picnic bathing parties, barbecues, birthday parties and our share of mumps, measles, chicken pox, scarlet fever and german measles.

There were cubs and scouts, junior bands, and judo and dancing classes. Trips to grandma in London and pantomimes, circuses and tournaments. There was always a mass of children in the house, plus friends and friends of friends. We were very lucky.

All three children first went to a local convent, up to the 11-plus examination. Trevor managed to pass this without too much trouble, Paul scrambled through by a miracle and Jane passed easily. This enabled the boys to go to the local grammar school and Jane to stay on at her convent without having to pay fees.

It meant that we didn't have to scrimp and save quite as much as my colleagues and could spend money on things like good holidays.

Whether we were right or wrong is difficult to say. Whenever we met the children of medical colleagues, not just our Tadchester partners but friends from medical school, Trevor and Paul felt exuded from the public school club. They used to think it all very funny and were great mimics.

Trevor was already established at grammar school when Jane went off for her first day at the convent: proud in her big red blazer and a satchel that almost dwarfed her, excited and serious, and with Pam keeping back the tears.

Ron Dickinson's daughter, Louise, was just a month younger than Jane and these two little tots used to go everywhere together and would be seen coming out from school with their huge satchels and huge blazers, holding hands, blonde pigtails sticking out at the back of their felt hats.

Trevor enjoyed school, pottering along at his own pace, watching it all from the distance. Paul hated it, apart from the sports, where he was always one of the team leaders. He much preferred to be lost in games of imagination, and at home he would race about as a pirate or a soldier, or run a gang from the old caravan we kept in the garden.

Jane loved school wholeheartedly and took part in every single school activity. She was always near the top of the form and seriously involved in whatever she was doing.

Trevor was very much the elder brother, totally dependable and always the first boy at school. He would set off at about 7.15 in the morning, walking three miles. I didn't even know if the school was open when he got there.

The age difference between the children was such that they

were not really in competition with one another. Jane, ten years younger than Trevor and six years younger than Paul, adored her brothers and they in turn thought they had the best little sister in the world and woebetide anybody who upset her.

School life went on serenely, apart from Paul's bad reports, until Trevor came to his first nightmare of O-levels. (I wonder if the examination system puts too much strain on our children and whether there is not some better way.)

Trevor worked solidly and hard, didn't ask for help, did well and got eight good O-levels.

There was a party to celebrate the results. That night we heard Trevor coming in late and crashing about more than usual. He wasn't very well the next day and when he'd gone to school we found a funny stain on the wall and the carpet. He'd been drunk for the first time and had come home, vomited and tried to clear it up. In the evening I asked him how he had got on the night before.

'Sorry, dad,' he said. 'I wasn't very well.'

'What had you been drinking?' I asked.

'Well,' he said, 'I don't like beer very much and I knew that you liked a glass of port. So I stuck to port — but I felt very funny.'

'How many glasses of port did you have?'

'Oh, about thirteen,' said Trevor. 'It does make your head swimmy after a time.'

Paul showed no interest in things academic. It was almost as if he had shut his mind off when any learning was floated in his direction, but he was captain of cricket and football, first the under-12s, then the under-13s, and so on. He was always organising, always busy.

Trevor and his friends could be members of the Sanford-on-Sea Golf Club for ten shillings a year. They made a profit on their subscriptions very quickly by caddying in the bigger matches and tournaments.

The golf course at Sanford-on-Sea was hazardous in that it was shared with people who had grazing rights in the area. You played golf in the company of rather wild horses, sheep, goats and any other thing that could get some nourishment from the sparse grass behind the natural pebble ridge breakwaters. Trevor came home once in tears, a great hole in his new golf bag. He had put it down at the edge of a green and a horse had chewed it.

He was a quiet, self-contained and happy boy. He worked hard towards his A-levels, and decided that he wanted to do law. He had an offer from Birmingham University and his master thought he should manage the grades comfortably. But his A-levels and the run-up to them were absolutely traumatic. He worked day and night and became a total wreck. We hardly dared make a noise in the house for three months.

When the results came he was completely distraught: he'd done much worse than he thought. His grades were one B, one D and an E; Birmingham wanted two Bs and a C so there was no chance of going there.

Dejectedly, Trevor started to ring and write to polytechnics to see if he could find a place at the last minute.

Of the polytechnics that did law Kingston appeared to be the best. They had a special course on criminology which he thought might be interesting. They wrote back to say that all the places were full, but perhaps he would like to try again next year. Trevor was heartbroken. 'I just can't go through A-levels again, dad. Now what shall I do?'

I said nothing would be lost if he wrote to Kingston again saying how much he wanted to go there; there was always a chance that someone would opt out. Trevor despatched his letter with little hope and began to scan the papers for job opportunities.

For his eighteenth birthday we had a little family party. A bottle of red wine and great big steaks, his favourite. As we sat down to eat, the phone rang: a call for Mr Trevor Clifford. It was Kingston Polytechnic, a vacancy had occurred and could he start the following Wednesday?

What a marvellous birthday present. Pam looked a bit downcast: it had just come home to her that the first of her chicks was about to fly the nest.

At last the day came for Trevor to go. We saw him off on the train with the usual last-minute advice about washing and brushing his teeth, and gave him some extra money so that if he really got fed up he could come home for a few days. He leaned out of the carriage window, a grinning face under a mop of fair hair, waving goodbye. Poor Pam had tears running down her cheeks and I felt just as bad.

'Come on, darling,' I said. 'Dry your eyes. He'll soon be home again.'

'I know he will,' said Pam, 'but I'm afraid that life is going to be different from now on.'

Postscript

There is the fable of the old man sitting outside a town, being approached by a stranger.

'What are they like in this town?' asked the stranger.

'What were they like in your last town?' replied the old man.

'They were delightful people. I was very happy there. They were kind, generous and would always help you in trouble.'

'You will find them very much like that in this town.'

The old man was approached by another stranger.

'What are the people like in this town?' asked the second stranger.

'What were they like in your last town?' replied the old man.

'It was an awful place. They were mean, unkind and nobody would ever help anybody.'

'I am afraid you will find it very much the same here,' said the old man.

If it should be your lot to ever visit Tadchester, this is how you will find us.

The hilarious, heartwarming tales of a GP in his West Country practice

SURELY NOT, DOCTOR!

Dr Robert Clifford

Doctor Bob's country practice is in Tadchester on the Somerset coast, but no one can accuse the town of being a sleepy little backwater. All human life is there with its quirks, colour, comedy and richness . . .

There's the absent-minded, incontinent vicar of St Peter's; the well-known London publisher whose dog has more taste than most . . . the lady magistrate who travels for miles for a doctor with warm hands and the packet of suppositories which prompts a bomb scare!

It all goes to show that truth can be so much stranger than fiction . . .

BIOGRAPHY/HUMOUR   0 7221 2386 8   £1.95

Don't miss Dr Robert Clifford's

JUST HERE, DOCTOR!
NOT THERE, DOCTOR!
WHAT NEXT, DOCTOR?
OH DEAR, DOCTOR!
LOOK OUT, DOCTOR!

Also available in Sphere Books

AN ENCHANTED LIFE
DEREK TANGYE
A QUIET YEAR

Derek Tangye's wish for a quiet year is fulfilled in this, the latest of the Minack Chronicles. In reflective mood he contrasts his and Jeannie's earlier life in London with the serenity of the daffodil farm, surrounded by animals and birds that make Minack so special.

0 7221 84018   AUTOBIOGRAPHY   £2.50

"Let's get back to Minack where our heart is, the embodiment of a dream."
DAILY TELEGRAPH

Get on yer bike!

GOB
Goods On Board

The hilarious new novel by
SIMON MAYLE

Dear Reader,

I promise you that this book is so witty you'll be reading it aloud to the nearest traffic warden. You'll need three boxes of extra-strong hankies for the sad bits. You'll find brilliant new insights into modern romance.

Besides all this, there's a load of great stuff about motorcycling, Life, and what it's like to wear leather.

Basically, reading this is nearly as good as doing a ton down the South Circular, or a wheelie along the Mall. Go for it!

James

0 7221 5750 9   GENERAL FICTION   £2.50

A selection of bestsellers from Sphere:

FICTION

THE SECRETS OF HARRY BRIGHT	Joseph Wambaugh	£2.95 ☐
CYCLOPS	Clive Cussler	£3.50 ☐
THE SEVENTH SECRET	Irving Wallace	£2.95 ☐
CARIBBEE	Thomas Hoover	£3.50 ☐
THE GLORY GAME	Janet Dailey	£3.50 ☐

FILM & TV TIE-IN

INTIMATE CONTACT	Jacqueline Osborne	£2.50 ☐
BEST OF BRITISH	Maurice Sellar	£8.95 ☐
SEX WITH PAULA YATES	Paula Yates	£2.95 ☐
RAW DEAL	Walter Wager	£2.50 ☐

NON-FICTION

URI GELLER'S FORTUNE SECRETS	Uri Geller	£2.50 ☐
A TASTE OF LIFE	Julie Stafford	£3.50 ☐
HOLLYWOOD A' GO-GO	Andrew Yule	£3.50 ☐
THE OXFORD CHILDREN'S THESAURUS		£3.95 ☐
THE MAUL AND THE PEAR TREE	T. A. Critchley & P. D. James	£3.50 ☐

All Sphere Books are available at your local bookshop or newsagent, or can be ordered direct from the publisher. Just tick the titles you want and fill in the form below.

Name_____

Address_____

_____

Write to Sphere Books, Cash Sales Department, P.O. Box 11, Falmouth, Cornwall TR10 9EN.

Please enclose a cheque or postal order to the value of the cover price plus: UK: 60p for the first book, 25p for the second book and 15p for each additional book ordered to a maximum charge of £1.90.

OVERSEAS & EIRE: £1.25 for the first book, 75p for the second book and 28p for each subsequent title ordered.

BFPO: 60p for the first book, 25p for the second book plus 15p per copy for the next 7 books, thereafter 9p per book.

Sphere Books reserve the right to show new retail prices on covers which may differ from those previously advertised in the text elsewhere, and to increase postal rates in accordance with the P.O.